A Research Guide for Health and Clinical Psychology

A Research Guide for Health and Clinical Psychology

Martin Dempster
Research Co-ordinator, DClinPsych Programme,
Queen's University Belfast

First published 2011 by
PALGRAVE MACMILLAN

Palgrave Macmillan in the UK is an imprint of Macmillan Publishers Limited,
registered in England, company number 785998, of Houndmills, Basingstoke,
Hampshire RG21 6XS.

Palgrave Macmillan in the US is a division of St Martin's Press LLC,
175 Fifth Avenue, New York, NY 10010.

Palgrave Macmillan is the global academic imprint of the above companies
and has companies and representatives throughout the world.

Palgrave® and Macmillan® are registered trademarks in the United States,
the United Kingdom, Europe and other countries.

ISBN 978–0–230–27919–3

This book is printed on paper suitable for recycling and made from fully
managed and sustained forest sources. Logging, pulping and manufacturing
processes are expected to conform to the environmental regulations of the
country of origin.

A catalogue record for this book is available from the British Library.

A catalog record for this book is available from the Library of Congress.

10 9 8 7 6 5 4 3 2 1
20 19 18 17 16 15 14 13 12 11

Printed and bound in Great Britain by
CPI Antony Rowe, Chippenham and Eastbourne

To my parents – my first teachers

Contents

Tables

Figures

Boxes

Acknowledgements

● ●

This book is based on questions that I have often been asked by health and clinical psychology trainees. Consequently, it could not exist without the probing, stimulating and challenging questions that trainees have asked me over the years. Their questions have caused me to question my thoughts and assumptions and have been a great source of professional development for me. Therefore, I must offer thanks to any trainee psychologist who has ever questioned their research process and who has asked me to help them find solutions. This thanks is not restricted to trainees but needs to be extended to my colleagues, to those psychologists who have asked me to help with their research dilemmas: I might not always have had the answers, but I was grateful for the questions!

The information provided in this book has been influenced by many people who have shaped my thinking about research. I enjoy research because of the people I have collaborated with and because of mentors and teachers who have encouraged my interest in the subject. These people are too many to mention, but they have contributed in some way to the information contained in this book.

Thanks needs to be extended to the reviewers who have helped to shape this book and to friends and colleagues who have provided some feedback on my initial ramblings. Thanks to Michelle Marshall for wading through the statistics and to Joanne Gallagher for allowing a part of her research to be included in this book. Special thanks to Noleen McCorry who provided feedback on several chapters of the book, was an endless source of support and encouragement and has helped to shape my thinking about research through our collaboration on a number of projects, including our collaboration in life, for which any words of acknowledgement are woefully inadequate.

1

The Role of Research in Health and Clinical Psychology

● ●

This book is a guide to assist trainee psychologists to demonstrate their competence in research as part of their training to become health psychologists or clinical psychologists. It is designed to apply equally to trainee psychologists following a university-based course and trainees following the independent route to training with the British Psychological Society. Although there are slightly different considerations depending on whether you are a trainee clinical psychologist or a trainee health psychologist undertaking a university-based course, or a trainee health psychologist taking the independent route, there is a considerable amount of similarity in the research experience of all these trainees.

This chapter discusses the reasons for the inclusion of research as an essential part of training for a health or clinical psychologist, some philosophical issues about research and some thoughts about the relationships that a trainee psychologist needs to establish and maintain during the course of a research project.

This chapter differs from the other chapters of the book. The remainder of the book provides some practical advice and guidance that will hopefully be useful when planning and conducting a research project. This chapter is mostly an attempt to encourage you to spend a little time reflecting on why you are being asked to engage in a research project, how this contributes to your personal and professional development, and why it is beneficial for the profession. In the other chapters of this book I attempt to answer questions that I have been asked by trainee health and clinical psychologists; in this chapter, I attempt to answer questions that I think *ought* to be asked by trainee health and clinical psychologists.

1.1 Psychologist versus researcher

When a student enrols for an undergraduate psychology programme, their expectations about the content of the programme are often not the same as the reality that awaits them. In short, many undergraduate psychology students expect that studying psychology means that they will be involved in 'treating' people with mental health problems. It can be disappointing when they find that this is not the case, even more disappointing when they realise that completing the undergraduate programme does not qualify them as a psychologist and potentially devastating when they find out that research methods and statistics constitute a compulsory part of the curriculum! (I think this situation is improving as 'school careers teachers' become more aware of the content of psychology programmes and a significant proportion of undergraduate psychology students have studied psychology at GCSE or A-level.)

Unfortunately, many undergraduate psychology students view the research components of their programme as a 'necessary evil' – something which they need to do to complete their qualification but something which they do not enjoy and do not want to remember for longer than necessary.

For a trainee psychologist enrolling on a postgraduate programme leading to qualification as a health or clinical psychologist, the research element of the curriculum comes as no surprise, but it still seems to sit uncomfortably with many trainees, perhaps as a consequence of the impressions formed as an undergraduate. I think the primary reason for this is that some trainees struggle to see the relevance of research in their training and others view the research element of their training as secondary to the other parts of their training, which constitute 'real psychology'. Undertaking postgraduate training in psychology means you will have little spare time and you will be required to prioritise goals and sometimes take a pragmatic approach. It is easy to see how the research can be sidelined, particularly when it spans a lengthy period, meaning the goals are not immediate and you have more urgent tasks, such as a client you are seeing tomorrow and for whom you really need to do some preparatory reading/thinking about your approach.

1.1.1   Why do psychologists need to conduct research?

I think this is a question which most trainee psychologists ask themselves at some point during their training, and if you are not in this category, then you ought to be. Unfortunately, this is not a question that many trainees will dwell on. I strongly encourage reflection on this question, preferably before enrolling on a postgraduate training programme. You are likely to reflect on the other aspects of your training – how they fit together and how they contribute to your knowledge and skills as a psychologist – so why should research be different? It is an integral part of your training and should be treated as such.

To contribute to your reflections about this question, here are some of my thoughts. I think research training is an important element of your training programme on the road to a clinical or health psychology qualification because it encourages the development of skills that are transferable across research and clinical settings; it helps you to interpret research findings, thereby ensuring your practice is evidence informed; it enables you to contribute to the psychological knowledge base; and it informs assessments of the quality of any psychological services you provide. These are important skills for any independent practitioner who intends to function at the level expected of a clinical or health psychologist, and they require a little more discussion.

1.1.1.1   Research training develops transferable skills

Some of the knowledge and skills that you accrue during your research training are specific to conducting a research project, but many are transferable across other aspects of your work as a psychologist, and, therefore, the research training should be considered a valuable professional development opportunity. For example, trainee health psychologists must meet the requirements of the generic professional unit of competence. This includes demonstrating an ability to, for example, practise within legal and ethical boundaries, communicate effectively, build alliances and engage in collaborative working, provide appropriate advice and guidance on concepts and evidence derived from health psychology, and lead groups or teams effectively. A list of nine transferable skills is highlighted by the accreditation criteria for clinical psychology training programmes. This is similar to the list referred to in the health psychology generic professional unit of competence and includes, for example, generalising and synthesising prior knowledge and experience in order to apply them critically and creatively in different settings and novel situations, and exercising personal responsibility and largely autonomous

initiative in complex and unpredictable situations in professional practice. All these abilities are required for the successful completion of a
research project and, therefore, your research training will contribute to
your generic professional development in similar ways to other aspects
of your training.

Furthermore, I encourage you to consider the similarities between
the research process and the process of psychological intervention.
Psychological intervention broadly consists of four elements: assessment,
formulation, intervention and evaluation. The assessment and formulation
process in a therapeutic setting is mirrored by the assessment of previous
research, identification of gaps in the literature and formulation of research
questions in a research setting. Similar skills are used in both settings –
the ability to seek out relevant information, synthesise this information,
formulate hypotheses on the basis of this information and then critically
evaluate these hypotheses to ensure they are appropriate. Choosing and
implementing an intervention in a therapeutic setting which is appropriate to the needs of the client and draws on your formulation is mirrored
by the process of choosing an appropriate research design and method
which is appropriate for the population being studied and derives from
the formulation of the research questions/hypotheses. Finally, evaluating
your therapeutic intervention mirrors the process in which your research
findings are evaluated in light of previous research and new research questions are generated and/or the original hypotheses are reformulated. I am
not suggesting that the research process and the therapeutic process are the
same, only that some similar skills are drawn upon.

1.1.1.2   Research training helps you evaluate research findings

In any service you deliver, it is important to ensure that you are providing clients with the most effective service that is reasonably practicable.
The standards of our profession demand this and the requirements for
continuous professional development aim to encourage this. But how do
you know that your service is as effective as it can be? The starting point
is to make sure that you employ the techniques and procedures which
have been shown to be effective by research evidence. This is not to suggest that you need to conduct this research, rather that you need to be
aware of the latest research that might inform your practice. The push for
evidence-based practice is strong in the medical field, leading to a plethora of guidelines about how patients should be treated. These guidelines
are meant to be evidence based in that they provide an indication of best
practice derived from good quality research evidence. The production of
these guidelines has also led to a plethora of clinical audits which aim to

determine whether health professionals are adhering to the latest guide-lines. Although there are debates about the appropriateness of clinical guidelines in some circumstances and the research designs that generate this evidence, the principle that patients/clients should be provided with the most effective care is a sound one.

In psychology, restricting ourselves to clinical practice which has a strong evidence base is, in my opinion, a step too far as it ignores the valuable role of the psychologist's experience, the inter-client variation which often renders a single standard procedure inappropriate and the fact that the effectiveness of some psychological interventions can be dif-ficult to demonstrate in the context of a controlled research environment. Furthermore, the constraint of evidence-based practice can stymie inno-vation. However, I advocate the notion that our practice should at least be evidence informed. That is, any psychological service that we provide should be informed by the most recent research findings. Therefore, psy-chologists need to keep abreast of the latest developments in the research literature and need to consider how these developments might influence their service provision. The research training that you undertake will help you to develop the knowledge and skills that will enable you to under-stand and critically evaluate the latest research information and to decide whether this information should affect your practice.

1.1.1.3   Research training enables you to make a contribution to psychological knowledge

This is probably the most obvious outcome from engaging in research training – successfully completing a research project is the best way of developing your skills and knowledge to conduct research in the future.

It is important that psychological research continues to inform psycho-logical practice. Our profession will remain static and become discredited in its absence. Good research has the potential to influence psychological practice only if applied psychologists are involved in the research process. The involvement of applied psychologists in the research process ensures, at least, that the practice implications of research findings are highlighted and that research questions relevant and timely for psychological practice are generated. Your research training will provide you with the knowledge and skills not only to contribute to this process, but to lead it.

1.1.1.4   Research training informs service evaluation

Service evaluation is important to ensure that the service you provide is having the desired impact on clients. The information generated through service evaluation is the minimum evidence that should be provided by a psychologist to suggest that their service is effective (see Chapter 8). The knowledge and skills that you develop through learning about research can be directly employed in this setting.

You will have encountered psychologists who do not appear to actively engage in research yet are respected in the profession. However, because a psychologist is not seen to be producing research papers does not mean that they are not using the research knowledge and skills derived from their training. Of course, the active production of research-based knowledge among psychologists is to be encouraged – who else is in a better position to generate data that will inform psychologists' practice? The production of research-based knowledge is not compulsory for psychologists, but, because of the requirements of continuous professional development and service quality assurance, the application of research knowledge and skills in their work is compulsory. The foundation for this knowledge and skills is laid during your training programme.

1.2   Thinking about research

It is important not only to consider why psychologists do research but also to consider why anyone does research. That is, what is the purpose of research? A consideration of this nature will lead us into the world of philosophy and epistemology.

1.2.1   Why is it important to consider epistemology?

It is useful for psychologists to visit the world of philosophy from time to time. In particular, a consideration of epistemology draws together the areas of research and philosophy and bridges the gap between the scientific practitioner and the reflective practitioner.

Epistemology is an examination of how we know that we know something, or, how knowledge is obtained. It is usually allied with ontology, which is an exploration of the nature of social reality. For example, you might take the ontological stance that reality is constructed in the interaction between people and does not exist outside this interaction. Consequently, you are also likely to take the epistemological stance that in order to understand a phenomenon, we must examine social interactions and the ways and means by which reality is constructed in interactions. This perspective will, in turn, obviously influence your choice of research design.

Epistemological approaches, broadly speaking, range from those which adopt a realist approach to those which adopt a relativist approach. The realist approach suggests that truth is an independent reality and that by careful experimentation we can discover this truth. This approach gives rise to the classical hypothesis-testing approach that undergraduate psychology students will be familiar with. The relativist approach holds that reality is somehow relative to something else. For example, a relativist approach might propose that a person's perception of an experience is relative to their cultural and family context, one person's perception might be different from another's, all perceptions are equally valid and worthy of understanding and, therefore, there is no one truth independent of these interactions. Relativists are likely to view experimental designs as an inappropriate approach for discovering information about these perceptions.

Within these broad epistemological approaches, there are a range of approaches where the differences are more subtle. Commonly discussed approaches in psychology are the positivist, post-positivist and social constructivist approaches. Positivists hold that the goal of science is to observe and measure phenomena. By doing this we can develop an understanding of the world. This assumes that phenomena operate in a deterministic fashion, and if we can theorise about these phenomena then we can develop and test hypotheses and refine our theories, in a process which will ultimately lead us to a true understanding of relationships between phenomena. When we think of scientists working in a laboratory on some physics/chemistry experiment, we are probably thinking of a positivist approach to research.

The post-positivist tradition (or more specifically, the critical realist tradition) is critical of the possibility that our observations and measurement will ultimately lead us to the truth. The critical realist believes that observations and measurement are prone to error and, therefore, truth may not be known with absolute certainty. The critical realist will also recognise the bias that researchers bring to their interpretations of information. In effect, critical realists believe that the truth is out there; it's just difficult and sometimes impossible to access.

Social constructivism posits that there is no single reality that can be studied, but that 'reality' is what an individual constructs through their interaction with the world. Social constructivism assumes that the researcher cannot be separated from the participant. In other words, the researcher does not gather data from a participant which represent that participant's experiences. Rather, the researcher plays a role in constructing the data as the data are a product of the interaction between the researcher and participant. The researcher is part of the life-world experienced by the research participant. This approach is discussed further in Chapter 7.

Although your epistemological stance does not equate to your choice of methodology (in the sense that different methodologies can be used by someone with a fixed epistemology), there are methodologies which flow from epistemological approaches logically and others which do not. Adopting a research design which does not fit logically with your epistemological approach might be one of the reasons you have found a research project in the past to be difficult to become enthused about. The dissonance might not have been obvious to you and you might have been left with a general dislike for research. Giving some consideration to your epistemological approach and to the type of research that sits comfortably with you is essential before choosing a research design. Even if the conclusion is that you have no strong epistemological pull in any direction and you are happy to take a pragmatic approach to research, the resolution of this in your own mind is a worthwhile exercise. A useful discussion of the relationship between epistemology and research methods is provided in chapter 1 of Mertens (2010).

Furthermore, without an understanding of epistemology, you will never be able to develop novel and innovative methods of conducting research. Instead, you will see research design as a list of options to be chosen from rather than as a set of examples of a potentially infinite number of research designs. Understanding the epistemology that underlies a research design is an attempt to understand the purpose of the research. Unfortunately, my experience of postgraduate psychology students is that their appreciation of epistemology is not good, and I imagine that this stems from the structure of research methods teaching in undergraduate psychology programmes. In my experience, research methods teaching in undergraduate psychology programmes in the UK is biased towards experimental designs and analysis of variance (ANOVA). There is no comparable coverage of other approaches and little discussion of the epistemological approach from which experimental designs tend to emanate.

1.2.2 What is the aim of research?

I have sometimes encountered trainees who are enthusiastic about their research project but become deflated or disappointed when they reach the analysis stage. I have also encountered trainees who become frustrated (more than I have come to expect) when their research project does not proceed as planned. Often this is because the trainee's expectations for the research are too high. In other words, the trainee has a slight misperception about the aim of research. Therefore, before embarking on a research project, I think it is worthwhile to contemplate the aim of research in general and the aim of your project in particular.

It is worth stating at the outset that we all encounter problems in our research, that we all have good ideas thwarted by circumstance and that we all experience frustration and disappointment on occasions as a result of research not proceeding as planned or as envisaged. The important thing is your response to these situations and your response will, probably, be largely based on your expectations.

Research is an investigation of some phenomenon which helps us to understand it better. When we understand something better than we did before, we are able to formulate more searching questions. Therefore, research will attempt to answer some questions but, by doing so, will raise additional questions. You should expect your research project to address specific questions satisfactorily but you should not expect the answers that you uncover to mark an end to the question. The aim of a research project is to provide the next chapter in an ongoing story. Your project will summarise the extent of our knowledge in an area to date, state the next logical question that needs to be addressed to further this knowledge, answer this question, and then indicate how your findings point us in the direction of further questions that need to be tackled. Your project might be a small part of the story, but it is an essential part.

Furthermore, the process of research is an uncertain one. You can plan carefully and diligently and, by doing so, you can avoid many problems that would otherwise prove fatal for your research project, but no amount of planning will prevent you encountering some unforeseen problem along the way. Being able to manage this uncertainty in the midst of the complexity of your research design and being able to develop novel solutions for problems encountered are two of the most important skills that a psychologist develops through their research training.

In summary, then, I think the aim of research is learning. Research outcomes help us to learn more about an area and to formulate questions to develop this learning; the research process helps us to learn about ourselves, how we respond to uncertain and complex situations and how we work as part of a research team.

1.3 Research collaboration

Most research is conducted by research teams, although in many cases the team might comprise only two people (you and a supervisor). The success or otherwise of research teams tends to be judged by their research outputs. However, good quality research outputs are unlikely to be produced by a dysfunctional team – the success of a research team depends as much on the management of inter-personal processes as it does on research-specific skills. Learning how to communicate effectively, develop your leadership role within a team and be a productive and collaborative team member are essential skills that you will develop throughout your training towards qualification as a psychologist. The research element of your training will contribute greatly to this development.

1.3.1 How do I choose a research supervisor?

The method of choosing, or being allocated, a research supervisor will depend on the specific procedures in place in your training programme. Many training programmes will allow the trainees to have some element of choice, but the choice of supervisor might very well be tied to the choice of research area. In many institutions, staff are assessed on the basis of their research output and are encouraged to be focused in their choice of research topics. Therefore, you might find that staff are prepared to agree to be your supervisor only if you are conducting research in areas which they have specified. In some training programmes, you will be permitted to identify your own research area, but there will then be an onus on you to identify, and secure the agreement of, a willing supervisor. Whatever the specific circumstance, it is likely that the choice of supervisor will in some way be coupled to your choice of research topic. Therefore, you need to find a topic in which you are interested and which will sustain your enthusiasm throughout the duration of the project (see Section 3.1).

As mentioned, in most training programmes you will have some degree of choice about who supervises you for your research project, but the reality is that this choice will probably be quite limited, and if you wish to conduct research in a specific area, you might find yourself with no choice at all. This is usually not problematic. If you are working with an experienced supervisor, you will find that they can adapt to the styles of different trainees and will be able to guide you through the process successfully.

1.3.2 What is my role in the research team?

Your role in the research team will largely be decided by the origins of your research project and by the point at which you joined the team. Some trainees will generate a research idea and be the drivers in the establishment of a research team; some trainees will join an existing team with a reasonably well developed research project; and many will join a research team which is somewhere between these two stages of development (often where a research idea has been suggested by someone but a team has not yet met in any formal sense to further this idea).

At first glance it might appear that joining a research team with a well developed project is beneficial and would lead to an easier transition through the research process. Yet there are some pros and cons that need to be considered.

- The research idea will have been developed by a research team who will probably have ensured that the research idea is feasible. However, this will prevent you from giving any input to the development of the research, and, by agreeing to join the research team, you will be obliged to follow the course already decided. Sometimes it will be obvious in a viva exam or project write-up that a trainee has joined an existing research project and has not really understood the development and conceptualisation of the project.
- The research team might be working to a different timetable than you would prefer. That is, you might be asked to undertake aspects of the research process at a time when you have other commitments on your training programme. It is likely that you will have little control over deadlines.
- The research team is likely to include all the relevant people necessary to ensure the success of the research project. This will be beneficial in that the people with whom you need to negotiate important elements of the project, such as access to participants, might already have indicated some willingness to be involved in the research.
- The research team will probably be able to assist with the analysis of the data, but they are also likely to have specific ideas about how the data should be analysed. This might require you to develop skills in data analysis that are beyond those required for your training programme.
- Some existing research teams will be sympathetic to your needs as a trainee and ensure that learning opportunities are provided for you during the course of the project. However, existing projects will probably have a tight time frame for completion (imposed by an outside agency), and therefore the focus of the research team might be the completion of the project and how you can speed this along. The danger here is that you become a research assistant rather than a trainee, devoting a considerable amount of time to the research but not availing of any potential development opportunities.
- If you join a research team that has already developed its idea to the point where data collection is almost ready to begin, then you have

a limited opportunity to contribute conceptually to the research project and, therefore, you are unlikely to be a senior author on any publication resulting from the project.

Whatever your role in the research team, it will be important for you to demonstrate that you are a competent researcher who can engage successfully in all aspects of the research process. If you have not actually been engaged in all aspects of the research process, this will be difficult to demonstrate, and you should consider the opportunities for this before joining a research team. For example, if you have not been involved in the original conceptualisation of the research project, then you might need to think of alternative methods of demonstrating your ability in this aspect of research. Re-conceptualising the project and being able to discuss alternative approaches to the research might be one method of doing this. Furthermore, it is your responsibility to ensure that the research report for your training programme is delivered on time and that it meets the requirements specified by your training programme. This responsibility cannot be delegated to other members of the research team.

1.3.3 What sort of help should I expect from a research supervisor?

A research supervisor's role is to assist and guide you in the development of your research knowledge and skills. The research supervisor's role is not to ensure that you successfully complete a research project – that is your responsibility. The research report that you submit is, therefore, a reflection of the research knowledge and skills that you have gained, not a reflection of your supervisor's knowledge and skills. If your collaboration with your research supervisor is underpinned with this understanding, then your expectations of the contribution from your supervisor are likely to be more realistic.

Research supervisors will be able to provide some guidance about how you can develop your research-specific knowledge and skills by pointing you towards useful sources of information and they will help you to reflect on the development of these skills. Research supervisors will also provide you with feedback on written work such as your research proposal and a draft of the research report (if you allow them sufficient time to do so). Two heads are better than one, and many heads are better still. Therefore, obtaining feedback from as many supervisors/collaborators as you can is beneficial. However, supervisors, assessors and other reviewers of research outputs will rarely agree on every aspect of the work that they review. In psychological research, it is appropriate for reviewers to have different opinions on how a research project should be conducted. Sometimes these disagreements will be minor; sometimes they will be more fundamental, but often they are not absolutely opposed. That is, reviewers might have different opinions about how a research project should be conducted, but they might also be prepared to accept each other's suggestions as valid. This occurs because there is no single correct approach to conducting a research project; there might be many equally valid ways of addressing the same issue. Consequently, it is inappropriate to expect the feedback you receive from different supervisors to match exactly. It is your responsibility to digest this feedback and to attempt to synthesise it. Remember, your supervisors are providing you with feedback which is an indication of their thoughts about your work and how it might be improved; they are not providing you with a list of revisions that you must make in order to make your work perfect. Complying with the feedback provided by your supervisors is no guarantee that the assessment outcome will be favourable – your supervisors are trying to improve your work, but the quality of the final product will depend on the quality of the initial product submitted to your supervisors for feedback. You should also remember that your supervisors are not infallible, and sometimes you might want to discuss the feedback they provide, especially if it does not make sense to you.

The help you receive from your supervisor will be specific to your supervisor. You should not expect all supervisors to have the same supervisory style – there are many valid approaches to research supervision. Standardisation is the refuge of the unimaginative and the characteristic of automatons. Psychologists should rejoice in individual differences.

The nature of the supervisor–supervisee relationship and the role of the supervisor will be governed, to some extent, by guidelines and regulations specific to the institution in which your training programme is located. You should make yourself aware of these.

1.3.4 *What should I do when things go wrong?*

Inevitably, problems will occur at some stage during the research process, and this is when the experience and advice of your supervisor will be most valuable. You need to bring any problems to the attention of your supervisor as early as possible. In general, the earlier a problem is identified, the greater the likelihood that it can be dealt with successfully.

This might seem like straightforward advice, but it is sometimes not followed in practice. Sometimes trainees will encounter problems with their research at a time when they are feeling overwhelmed with other aspects of their workload. In these situations it is very tempting to ignore the non-immediate problem (which is usually the research-related problem) and deal with the other pressing deadlines. I think this is because these trainees feel that they cannot control research-related problems and so it is easier to focus on work they can control. When you experience feelings such as a lack of control over the research process, that should set off the alarm that tells you to speak to your supervisor. The appropriate response to encountering a difficult problem is to deal with the challenge and develop a strategy for negotiating a way around this; avoiding the problem is likely to compound it.

Unfortunately, on the rare occasion, things can go wrong so drastically that a complete rethink of the research project is required. My aim, and the aim of your supervisor, is to ensure that this does not happen. The chances of this happening will decrease considerably by careful consideration and planning at each step in the process. I hope that the remainder of this book will assist you in these considerations.

1.4 Summary

In this chapter, I have discussed the role of research in the training of health or clinical psychologists, the purpose of research and the formation and management of research collaborations.

I have argued that research training is an important element in the knowledge and skills development of trainee psychologists because it encourages the development of skills that are transferable across research and clinical settings; it helps you to interpret research findings, thereby ensuring your practice is evidence informed; it enables you to contribute to the psychological knowledge base; and it informs assessments of the quality of any psychological services you provide.

I have also suggested that considering your epistemological approach and reflecting on what it is realistic to achieve within the constraints of your research project are useful exercises to engage in prior to and during the research process. Such reflections are likely to result in more appropriate research designs and more appropriate expectations about the research report.

Finally, I have outlined the types of expectations that you should and should not have about your research supervisor and the expectations about your role in this research collaboration.

2

Systematic Literature Reviews

● ●

Under current requirements for a British Psychological Society (BPS) accredited qualification in health psychology, trainee health psychologists are required to conduct a systematic review. Although this is not an explicitly stated requirement in the BPS accreditation criteria for postgraduate clinical psychology courses, most clinical psychology training programmes will expect their trainees to undertake a literature review which will, to a greater or lesser extent, comply with the guidelines for conducting a systematic review.

2.1   What are systematic reviews and why are they useful?

2.1.1   What are systematic reviews?

A systematic review is a comprehensive review of literature which differs from a traditional literature review in that it is conducted in a methodical (or systematic) manner, according to a pre-specified protocol to minimise bias, with the aim of synthesising the retrieved information, often using statistical tests (meta-analysis).

A systematic review aims to answer a specific question by identifying as much as possible of the research literature relevant to this question and then summarising the important information from this body of literature. Systematic reviews normally proceed as follows: identify the need for a review; specify the review question; define the search strategy and conduct the literature search; assess the eligibility of retrieved articles;

extract relevant data from the relevant articles; assess the quality of the relevant articles; synthesise the data; and disseminate the findings. Each of these stages of the systematic review process will be discussed in detail in the remainder of this chapter.

2.1.2 Why do it?

The obvious answer is because you need to in order to obtain your qualification as a health or clinical psychologist. However, these training requirements are in place to ensure that as a health psychologist or as a clinical psychologist, you are able to critically review literature in an area in order to answer a question which may inform your practice or future research. For example, as a practicing psychologist you may want to know the most appropriate type of intervention to use to address the depression being experienced by women with breast cancer. Perhaps the best way of finding this would be to examine the research literature that has evaluated relevant interventions among the population of women with breast cancer. Having the skills to retrieve the research in this area, weighing up the evidence presented in the research and drawing conclusions will have important implications for your practice. Therefore, this competence is very important in the world of clinical practice in addition to the world of research.

Indeed, systematic reviews have become very important in informing the practice of health professionals. They often form the basis of practice guidelines and inform health policy (such as guidance issued by NICE: http://www.nice.org.uk/). Although this push towards 'evidence-based practice' is not welcomed by everyone as it takes a very narrow view of what constitutes 'good' evidence, there is no reason to believe that this approach to decision making will change in the near future.

A systematic review is an important piece of research in its own right. You may decide to (be required to) conduct a systematic review as a stand-alone piece of work, or you may decide to conduct a systematic review in an attempt to highlight the need for a primary research study. Although it is not necessary to do a systematic review before developing a research proposal (a comprehensive non-systematic review is more often than not what happens), conducting a review in this manner can increase your confidence about the need for the research question and is always more convincing for examiners. Indeed, making a case for obtaining funding for a piece of research is often strengthened if the rationale is based on a systematic review.

2.2 The review protocol

2.2.1 Where do I start?

Like any good piece of research, it is important to invest time in the planning stage. This is when most of your thinking is done, and the time
spent here can be fruitful in identifying future problems and solutions.
Therefore, when undertaking a systematic review, the researcher should
produce a systematic review protocol. In fact, these protocols are often
published to ensure that no-one else begins a similar review at the same
time, and are peer reviewed to make sure the review will be conducted
in an appropriate manner. Therefore, it may be worthwhile examining databases of review protocols to ensure that no-one else is currently
doing the review that you are thinking of doing and to see some examples of how review protocols are written. Systematic review protocols are
published by organisations such as the Cochrane Collaboration (http://
www.cochrane.org/reviews/en/index_list_all_protocols.html) and the
Campbell Collaboration (http://www.campbellcollaboration.org/library.
php). These organisations and others such as the Centre for Reviews
and Dissemination (http://www.crd.york.ac.uk/crdweb/) also provide
abstracts of completed systematic reviews, so you can check whether or
not someone has recently completed a review in the area you were thinking about.

Spending time with your supervisor in the careful construction of a
review protocol will be time well spent. It provides a useful plan of work
and can often include a timetable and a list of individuals' responsibilities. All the components of the protocol should be piloted before embarking on the data collection phase of the review. The protocol enables you
to consider the type of people that needs to be included in the review
team, it provides a focus for the team, it allows an assessment of the time
required for the review and it publicises the plans for the review.

The protocol should contain the following information: the title of
the systematic review; the background and rationale for the review; the
review question; the eligibility criteria; the planned search strategies; the
quality criteria; and the plans for data extraction, analysis and dissemination. These will be dealt with in the following sections.

2.2.2 What should a systematic review question look like?

A systematic review aims to answer a specific and focused question.
A general guideline for formulating the question is that a systematic

review cannot answer questions that could not be answered using primary research. For example, a systematic review might aim to answer the question: 'what is the association between dietary self-efficacy and dietary behaviour among obese people?' or 'what are the experiences of health care services among people who are diagnosed with Parkinson's Disease?' or 'is mindfulness-based cognitive therapy effective in reducing levels of depression?' The last of these questions is a question about the effectiveness of an intervention, and some guidelines suggest that when developing a review question that focuses on effectiveness, you should structure your question using the PICO acronym. PICO stands for Participants, Intervention, Comparison and Outcomes. In other words, your review question should specify who the participants are, what the intervention is, with whom comparisons will be made and how effectiveness will be assessed. This can result in a lengthy but focused question. For our example, using the PICO approach could result in the following question: 'when used among adults with a diagnosis of depression who have been referred to an adult mental health service, is mindfulness-based cognitive therapy more effective at reducing levels of self-reported depression than bibliotherapy?'

Formulating an appropriate review question is probably the issue that, in my experience, causes the greatest problems for trainee psychologists when conducting a systematic review. If you have never conducted one before it can be difficult to get to grips with the level of specificity required for the question and how this impacts on the conduct of your systematic review. The problem is that you are expected to develop a focused question which will be appropriate for a systematic review before you have conducted a review. Yet a good knowledge of the literature is helpful when developing the question. The seemingly back-to-front nature of the process can cause understandable confusion!

The solution is to conduct a mini-review of the literature (often called a scoping review) to get a feel for the type of literature and amount of literature that exists in your topic of interest. You will be able to develop an appropriate review question only after you have armed yourself with this knowledge. Primarily the mini-review will help you to develop a review question which is feasible. You may have an idea for a systematic review question, but if there is no primary research that has addressed this question then it is not possible to conduct a systematic review in the area. On the other hand, you may find that there has been a large amount of literature that falls within the scope of your idea (too much literature to review in the time frame available), and therefore your review question needs to become more focused. You need to set the parameters of your review according to available resources. There is no point in aiming to do a very ambitious piece of research and then failing to do it adequately; there is also no point in conducting a piece of research which does not answer a substantive question. So the level of specificity and focus of your review question needs to be tailored to the time and other resources you have, without becoming so narrowly focused that it does not make a useful contribution to the area of knowledge. This is a difficult balancing act, and the experience of your supervisor and/or other psychologists working in the area will be valuable in helping you with this decision-making process.

For many trainees, the process works as follows: identify an area of interest; identify a topic within your area of interest where a review and synthesis of existing literature would be helpful; conduct a mini-review of this topic and then focus the question appropriately. For example, you may find that the question 'what is the association between dietary self-efficacy and dietary behaviour among obese people' will result in the identification of lots of research articles, but if we refine this question to 'what is the association between dietary self-efficacy and fat intake among obese people' then this will result in fewer research articles.

Notice the vagueness (lots of articles vs fewer articles)? Most trainees do when I use this type of language and the predictable question is: how many articles should be included in a review? Or how do I know when I have reached an appropriate level of focus? I really don't like answering this question because the answer is not satisfactory for trainees. That is, it would make your life easier if I just gave a number here, but that would be misleading. Indeed, you have probably realised that the lack of simple answers is a recurring theme in psychology, so why should research in psychology be any different? Psychologists should be comfortable with complexity – it's probably one of the most important attributes we can develop in our training. So, to return to the question, it will not surprise you when I say that the route to finding the answer to this question is a complex one. (The corollary is when trainees ask how many participants are needed in a primary research study; there is no single answer and the answer depends on a number of factors. See power calculations in Section 3.2.) If you look at published systematic reviews, you will see a range of articles included, from reviews of three studies upwards. So this brings me back to the previous point – if there is a good rationale for the review question and there are some articles to review, then the review should be appropriate. Also, you need to take into consideration the time you have available. In my experience, trainees who do good systematic reviews usually include a number of studies in the range of 5–15. The higher numbers are usually reserved for reviews of quantitative research where a meta-analysis is possible. In the cases where a narrative synthesis is conducted, the number tends to be towards the lower end of the range (see Section 2.4). However, I feel I need to reiterate that the number of studies is not the target of the review, and the number of studies reviewed should be dictated by the focus of the review question, which must have a clear rationale.

2.2.3 How do I find the research studies that address my review question?

Articles for the review can be retrieved by searching electronic databases, by hand searching through appropriate journals and by contacting researchers in the area of interest. To avoid bias in the retrieval of articles, in much the same way as we wish to avoid bias in the selection of a sample for primary research, the search strategy specified in the protocol must include as much detail as possible. In most cases this amounts to a list of keywords and how they will be combined for use in electronic search engines. Some knowledge of the capability of each subject-specific database is important at this point, as some databases operate a thesaurus search system and others operate on the basis of keywords only. For this reason, the assistance of an information specialist (a friendly librarian with experience of using relevant electronic literature databases) is helpful during the early stages of a systematic review.

Electronic searches are now the most common method of searching for literature for systematic reviews or, at least, are the starting point for these searches. Electronic databases commonly used by health and clinical psychologists are PsychINFO, Web of Science (within Web of Knowledge), MEDLINE (Medical Literature Analysis and Retrieval System Online) and CINAHL (Cumulative Index to Nursing and Allied Health Literature). The search strategy specified should be specific to the electronic database as different databases use different methods of searching. In some respects, the PsychINFO, MEDLINE and CINAHL databases are similar, as they have a thesaurus facility, although the thesaurus terms differ among the databases. The benefit of a thesaurus is that it will identify studies with similar keywords to the ones that you have identified as important for your search strategy.

The Web of Science database uses a keyword search with Boolean algebra (which is also available on the other databases). This means that you need to think of all possible terms that could be used to describe your topic of interest. Boolean algebra is a method of combining these search terms using the AND, OR, or NOT functions. Let's look at, for example, the question: 'what is the association between dietary self-efficacy and dietary behaviour among obese people?' To address this question we would want to find literature that included information on dietary self-efficacy and dietary behaviour and obese people. Let's say we want to initially find all the research articles that contain information about dietary behaviour. If using Web of Science, we could search using the following search terms:

Diet* OR eat*

The inclusion of the * is a method of truncating words and means that the search engine will search for any word beginning with that stem. For example, using the search term diet* will include articles that include the word diet or dietary or diets or dieting. It should be clear from this that it is important to identify all possible variants of the term under investigation. Conducting this search may result in a lot of articles about eating behaviour in rats (not unusual in psychology), so you will want to exclude these articles from your search, using the 'NOT' term:

(Diet* OR eat*) NOT rats

You will then want to further restrict this search to articles about self-efficacy, resulting in the search term:

((Diet* OR eat*) NOT rats) AND (self efficac* OR self-efficac*)

Of course, the length of your search term will be determined by the number of variants of each topic and by the number of topics that need to be addressed.

When using a thesaurus facility, you are selecting a term which represents a topic included in the article rather than searching for a specific word included in an article. For example, on PsychINFO, if you wished to search for articles on dietary behaviour, you would select the thesaurus term 'eating behaviour'. This includes articles on eating, eating habits, eating patterns and feeding practices. The thesaurus will also inform you about more narrowly focused terms that come under this heading (for example, dietary restraint) and give you the option of including these terms in your search.

There is a skill in using electronic databases, and the idiosyncrasies of different databases are too detailed to be covered in this book. For example, some databases use a $ symbol rather than the * to indicate word truncation and some databases require double quotation marks to enclose a search phrase, for example, self efficacy. Therefore, it is important to make yourself familiar with the nuances of any electronic database that you will be using by consulting its online help system.

The specification of the search strategy is a very important step in the systematic review, and if it is not given due consideration, the results of the literature search and, therefore, the conclusions of the review can be biased and, at best, unhelpful. The problem here is that people will often launch a search for literature and attempt to refine the search strategy as they are doing it. It is much more likely that literature will be missed using this approach rather than when using an approach where a group of people (perhaps only the trainee and their supervisor) consider the alternative search terms and the implication of using these terms and perhaps engage in some trial and error assessments of the effect of combining terms on individual databases. Ultimately, your choice of the search terms you use and which electronic databases to search should aim for a search outcome which is highly sensitive and specific, that is a search outcome that identifies the relevant articles without including many irrelevant articles. Sensitivity of a search refers to the proportion of relevant studies identified, and specificity of a search refers to the proportion of studies identified that are relevant (see Table 2.1). Spending time refining your search strategy to ensure that it optimises sensitivity and specificity will save you time reading through irrelevant articles later. However, a comprehensive systematic review will tend to prioritise sensitivity over specificity, meaning that in order to reduce the chances of missing relevant research, you are likely to obtain a number of irrelevant articles in your search.

$$\text{Specificity (or Precision)} = A\ /\ A{+}C \qquad \text{Sensitivity} = A\ /\ A{+}B$$

The actual search terms are often included in the published review and if applied to the databases, should replicate the outcome of the search. So you need to do this carefully and note any changes you make to the final search.

Finally, you may decide to conduct hand searches for literature that might have been missed in the electronic search. This usually refers to looking through the reference lists of the articles identified by the search of the electronic databases to ensure that you have any relevant material cited.

Table 2.1 Sensitivity and specificity

	Identified by search	Missed by search
Relevant	A	B
Irrelevant	C	D

2.2.4   Should I review everything that I can find on the topic?

The short answer is probably not. Research studies within the same area will use different research designs to answer (sometimes only slightly) different research questions. The quality of this research can also vary greatly. You need to make a decision about the type of research that will be included in your review (often referred to as eligibility criteria) and the minimum level of quality that a research study should meet before it is included in your review (often referred to as the quality or validity criteria). You also need to decide on what type of information will be extracted from the studies included in the review. Let's look at each of these in turn.

2.2.4.1   Eligibility criteria

You must decide what types of study design will be included in the review. For example, if the review aims to assess the effectiveness of an intervention, you may decide that only studies following a randomised controlled trial design will be acceptable. You also need to decide whether the review should be restricted to peer-reviewed, published material or whether you should be trying to gather any research conducted in your area, such as that published in reports or theses (often referred to as the 'grey' literature), or research which has not been published (which you can obtain directly from the researcher). Opting not to include these sources of information can potentially result in a review being influenced by publication bias (see the section on publication bias in this chapter).

In addition, the eligibility criteria should address issues such as the acceptable types of setting, participant, intervention and comparator, outcome and any language or date restriction. In effect, the eligibility criteria are an elaboration or operationalisation of the terms and parameters of your review question. They are analogous to the specification of inclusion/exclusion criteria in primary research. Therefore, the restrictions placed on the review by the eligibility criteria should be justified.

A question often asked at this point by trainees is whether it is appropriate to include a mixture of qualitative and quantitative research in a single systematic review and/or whether it is appropriate to include a mixture of primary research and existing literature reviews in a single systematic review.

Let's deal with the quantitative/qualitative mix first. Remember that the aim of a systematic review is to synthesise different research studies which have addressed the same question, thereby providing us with an answer to the question based on a critical analysis of the currently available evidence. Research which is based on quantitative data tends to address different questions than research based on qualitative data. Of course, you will find research studies that use both qualitative and quantitative data, but these data are used to answer (at least subtly) different questions within the same study. It is not surprising, therefore, that the vast majority of systematic reviews will not include a mixture of qualitative and quantitative evidence. But it is not impossible, and there are good reasons for encouraging a broader approach to the types of study included in systematic reviews. It is possible that you could formulate your review question in such a way that it would encompass results from both qualitative and quantitative research, and there are some who would recommend this approach (for example, Dixon-Woods & Fitzpatrick, 2001). However, I have always advised trainees against this course of action primarily because I think that the synthesis of data extracted from a mixture of qualitative and quantitative research is a more complex and time-consuming activity than the synthesis of data extracted from either quantitative research only or qualitative research only. Therefore, my advice here is couched within the constraints and demands of training towards qualification as a health or clinical psychologist and is pragmatic rather than being based in epistemology.

Second, I would caution against mixing the data extracted from primary research with that extracted from previous reviews in a single review. This is mainly because when you are using data extracted from a previous review, you are obtaining the data from a secondary source, and it is always possible that a secondary source can misrepresent (unintentionally) the findings that were reported in the primary source. So I would always advise returning to the primary source and taking the data from there. Additionally, you need to ask yourself whether there is a need for your systematic review if a review of the same topic has already been published. Often it is the case that a review was published some time ago and a considerable amount of research has been published since and therefore there is a need for your review to update our knowledge in the area. But bear in mind that authors of systematic reviews will often revisit the literature periodically to update their reviews. Whatever the case, you need to be clear about the rationale for your review.

2.2.4.2   Quality criteria

Having decided on the type of studies to be included in the review, you should now decide how the validity (or quality) of each study is to be assessed, because even published research can be poorly designed, analysed, interpreted or reported. Basically, quality criteria are a list of characteristics that a study should possess if it has been conducted in a rigorous manner. The characteristics that indicate quality in study design are discussed in Chapters 4 and 6. The quality criteria are a method of indicating the level of rigour or quality of a particular research study. The quality criteria will depend greatly on the types of study to be included in the review, however, quality checklists have been published for the assessment of many types of quantitative and qualitative research, and these might be useful in the development of quality criteria for your review. (See Elliott, Fischer & Rennie, 1999; Barbour, 2001; Meyrick, 2006 for discussions about quality in qualitative research. See http://www.ephpp. ca/tools.html; Zaza et al., 2000 for examples of checklists for quantitative research.)

In some published reviews you will find that the authors have provided a score for the quality of each research article reviewed (based on their quality criteria) and then incorporated this score into the meta-analysis (see Section 2.4.3). In other reviews, authors will exclude articles which do not meet some pre-determined quality threshold (as a way of ensuring that the conclusions of the review are based on high quality evidence). However, you might choose to use the quality criteria to assist you to develop a sense of how well the research studies were conducted, which will feed into your critical appraisal of the research included in your systematic review.

2.2.4.3   Data extraction, analysis and dissemination

A data extraction form is a form designed to prompt you to look for the relevant information within a research study that is needed for the review and provides space for you to record this information. In this way, the same information is extracted from each research study, and this information is then in a more accessible format when it comes to conducting the data synthesis/analysis. For example, a data extraction form for quantitative studies might include the following information: study identifier, details of the study design, number of participants (in each group if appropriate), descriptive statistics about participants (age, sex, etc.), name of the outcome measures, mean and standard deviation scores on each outcome measure, and other relevant statistics.

The content of a data extraction form will depend very much on the type of review to be undertaken. For example, a data extraction form and plan of analysis can easily be designed and included in a protocol for reviews which are intended to include only one type of study design. Yet with more complex reviews the data extraction form will begin broadly and will be amended as the variety of information provided by the different types of study becomes apparent. Whatever the case the protocol should contain some information about the type of data that will be sought during the review (based on a consideration of the users of the review), whether the synthesis of information will be narrative, statistical, or a combination of both and how the results will be reported (see Zaza et al., 2000 for an example of a comprehensive data extraction form).

2.3   Conducting the review

In many ways, conducting the review is the easiest part of the process. If you have spent time developing and refining your protocol, then it is simply a matter of following this plan. Nevertheless, some important issues arise during the course of the review, and the following sections might help to address these.

2.3.1   How do I find the relevant articles within the literature retrieved?

As implied in Section 2.2, no matter how well-refined your search strategy is, it is unlikely that it will identify only relevant articles. When you run your search terms in the electronic databases, the articles returned (often called 'hits') will hopefully include all the articles you are looking for, but these will probably be mixed with a number of irrelevant articles. The proportion of hits which are irrelevant will vary depending on how clearly and unambiguously your topic of interest is indexed in the electronic databases you are searching. The upshot is that you will need to read through the retrieved articles to determine whether they are relevant to your review. That is, you will need to apply your eligibility criteria to every hit.

If your search has retrieved a large number of articles, then it would be very time consuming and costly to obtain the full text of every article retrieved and read through it to determine its relevance to your review question. On the assumption that a proportion of these articles will be obviously irrelevant, you could begin by applying your eligibility criteria to the abstracts of each article (which are provided in the electronic databases). This assessment will result in one of three outcomes:

1. The article appears to meet the eligibility criteria – obtain the full text.
2. The article does not meet the eligibility criteria – do not include.

3. There is not enough information in the abstract to make a decision about whether the article meets the eligibility criteria or not – obtain the full text.

When you have obtained the full text of the reduced number of articles, you can then apply your eligibility criteria to the full text. In this case also the assessment will result in one of three outcomes:

1. The article is relevant as it meets the eligibility criteria – include in the review.
2. The article is irrelevant because it does not meet the eligibility criteria – do not include.
3. Unsure about relevance.

When your decision falls into category 3, then it is important to discuss the decision with another reviewer (your supervisor?) and reach an agreement on whether the article should be included in the review. If an agreement cannot be reached between you and the other reviewer, then a third person could be called in to consider the issues and facilitate agreement. It is good practice to have two reviewers independently reviewing the retrieved articles, to minimise bias in the outcomes.

One of the most important things to do when conducting the review is to keep a record of everything you have done. In particular, it is important to keep a record of the number of hits on each database and the outcomes of the assessment of relevance at both the abstract and full text stage, along with reasons for the exclusion of articles. This will not only allow you to clearly write up the process of the systematic review but also to evaluate the process. For example, after the two reviewers have made their decisions about each article on the basis of abstracts, you should consider the extent to which the two reviewers agree in their decision making. If their decisions are not similar then this may indicate some misunderstandings on the part of one or both reviewers about how to interpret the eligibility criteria. This would highlight the need for the reviewers to discuss and remedy this before progressing. Formal assessment of the reviewers' level of agreement can be conducted using a kappa (Cohen, 1960) or a weighted kappa statistic (see Taylor, Dempster & Donnelly, 2003 for an example of this process).

The kappa statistic is a statistic which assesses the level of agreement between two raters, where the outcome is categorical (for example, yes/no/don't know). If you want to assess the level of agreement between two reviewers in terms of the three outcomes mentioned above (relevant/irrelevant/unsure), then weighted kappa might be appropriate. Weighted kappa assumes that the outcome categories are ordered. In this example, weighted kappa is useful because it weights the responses so that a decision of 'relevant' is considered to be more different from a decision of 'irrelevant' which in turn is more different than a decision of 'unsure'.

As an example of the calculation of these statistics, let us assume we have retrieved 200 articles from our search. Two reviewers then independently assess the relevance of these articles on the basis of the abstracts. After completing this assessment, reviewer 1 believes that 100 articles are relevant, 20 are irrelevant and the reviewer is unsure about the remaining 80. Reviewer 2 believes that 80 articles are relevant, 30 are irrelevant and this reviewer is unsure about the remaining 90. The overlap between the reviewers' decisions is shown in Table 2.2.

We can determine the reviewers' level of agreement by examining the values in the cells along the diagonal of the table (the cells circled). As the two reviewers agreed to include 70/200 articles, agreed to exclude 15/200 articles and agreed that they were unsure about 68/200 articles, we could report that the agreement rate was (70+15+68)/200 = 153/200 or 76.5 %. However, this over-estimates the level of agreement, as it does not take into consideration that some of these agreements will occur by chance. Kappa does take account of this by comparing the agreement rate (observed agreement) with the agreement rate you would expect to get by chance (expected agreement). The calculation for the expected agreement and kappa is provided in Box 2.1. Kappa ranges from 0 to 1, where a value of 1 indicates perfect agreement. There are many rules of thumb about interpreting values of kappa, but these are not really important in this situation. Here, kappa is being used to highlight discrepancies between reviewers which can then be resolved through discussion, and I suggest that any kappa value below 0.8 indicates the need for some discussion.

Alternatively, the data presented in Table 2.2 could be analysed using weighted kappa, if you believe the responses are ordered (and this would be

Table 2.2 Assessing agreement between reviewers

		Reviewer 1			
		Include (n)	Unsure (n)	Exclude (n)	Row total
Reviewer 2	Include (n)	(70)	7	3	80
	Unsure (n)	20	(68)	2	90
	Exclude (n)	10	5	(15)	30
	Column total	100	80	20	200

appropriate here). The calculation for weighted kappa is a little more complex but, unlike kappa, it is not available on the most commonly used statistical software package in psychology – SPSS. Nevertheless, Fleiss and Cohen (1973) have shown that the intra-class correlation coefficient (which is available on SPSS) provides a value which is equivalent to weighted kappa.

Finally, in terms of dealing with the outcome of your search strategy, I would strongly recommend that you become familiar with and make use of a bibliographic management tool. There are a number of these tools (such as RefWorks, EndNote, RefMan), and your institution may well have a subscription to one you can use. These tools are invaluable when conducting systematic reviews. The articles retrieved from electronic databases (including the abstracts) can be downloaded into the bibliographic management software, and you can then ask the software to create reference lists for you, among other useful functions.

Box 2.1   Calculating Kappa

To calculate the expected agreement levels for kappa, calculate the following for each cell on the diagonal of the table (the circled cells):
(row total x column total) / total n
  Applying this to Table 2.2,
  (80 x 100)/200 = 40 expected agreements for 'include'
  (90 x 80)/200 = 36 expected agreements for 'unsure'
  (20 x 30)/200 = 3 expected agreements for 'exclude'
  Therefore, we would expect a total of 79/200 agreements by chance.
Kappa = the difference between total observed and total expected agreements divided by the total expected disagreements:
(total observed – total expected) / (total n – total expected)
  For Table 2.2, this is
  (153–79)/(200–79) = 74/121 = 0.612

2.3.2   What information should be extracted from the articles included in the review?

Once the irrelevant articles (that is, those articles not meeting the eligibility criteria) have been removed, you then need to synthesise the information contained in the remaining set of articles. At this stage, it might be helpful to extract the information that you need from each article and store it in a separate file. Doing this will mean that the important information is readily accessible (rather than buried within the context of each article) and it will be easier to draw it together in your write-up. There are two types of information that you will need to extract from each article: information about the research quality and the data that directly address the review question. We will look at each in turn.

2.3.2.1 Quality assessment

Again, assessing articles for quality is a matter of applying the quality criteria developed at the protocol stage. If time has been spent considering these criteria, then time will be saved when it comes to applying them. As with the eligibility assessment, the quality assessment should be conducted independently by two reviewers and their level of agreement assessed statistically (where the number of articles is sufficiently large to permit this).

The type of information extracted for the quality assessment will depend on the decision of the review team about what this information will be used for. For example, the team could decide to use the quality criteria to assign a quality score to each article. This score can then be treated in a number of ways, such as incorporating the quality score as a weighting factor in the meta-analysis phase, or excluding articles from the review on the basis of an a priori decision on a quality cut-off score (see Taylor, Dempster & Donnelly, 2007). However, reducing the interplay between different elements of study quality to a single score can, in some cases, be detrimental to our understanding of the standing of research in the area of the review. In these situations, it may be better to grade articles in terms of higher and lower quality (and discuss the meaning of these grades within the context of the review) and synthesise the data obtained from each category of articles separately. Although this may still be considered a reductionist approach, it is useful to provide readers of a review with an indication about which study findings should be given more weight (the higher quality studies), especially when study findings are contradictory. By its nature, a systematic review is reductionist. So by undertaking a systematic review, you are accepting that some degree of summary is required.

2.3.2.2 Obtaining data

Extracting relevant data (either qualitative or quantitative) from your articles is an attempt to reduce the information presented in each article to a manageable amount of information which will be included in the review analysis. The nature of the data extracted will depend on the review question. Where quantitative data is to be extracted, this will normally take the form of information about sample sizes, means, standard deviations (or other appropriate summary statistics), test statistics, p values and effect sizes (and a standard data extraction form can be useful here). Where qualitative data is to be extracted, the form of this data can be considerably more variable. Primarily, you need to ensure that you have extracted the data needed to complete your synthesis, so that you don't need to continually revisit articles to get another piece of information. Therefore, you need to be clear (in your protocol) about whether a narrative synthesis and/or meta-analysis will be conducted and if so, using what type of data.

Again, continuing the theme of reducing bias in the process of the systematic review, data extraction should be conducted independently by two reviewers.

When extracting data, reviewers must be wary of duplicate publications – the same study reported in different formats in different sources. This can be something as simple as retrieving the same article from more than one electronic database. Or it could be something more subtle. For example, it may be that a longitudinal study has been undertaken by researchers, and they have published the baseline cross-sectional data in one paper and then the longitudinal findings in another paper. In this case, the baseline data are repeated, so you need to be wary of including this information twice.

Furthermore, sometimes you will find that studies do not report sufficient detail about the type of result you are seeking. These studies should not be discarded, but some attempt should be made to contact the study authors in order to retrieve the necessary detail. With quantitative research you should bear in mind that sometimes studies will not report the exact statistics you are seeking, but they will report sufficient information to allow you to calculate these statistics. For example, you may need the standard deviation statistic for a sample to calculate an effect-size statistic (see Section 2.4), but the standard error is included in the study in preference to the standard deviation. Knowing that the standard deviation is the standard error multiplied by the square root of the sample size ($SD = SE \sqrt{n}$) means that you can get what you need. Obviously, the help of your supervisor and/or a statistician will be valuable here and when it comes to performing any meta-analysis.

2.4 Synthesising and disseminating the data

Once the relevant data have been extracted from the relevant articles, all that remains is to synthesise the data and report your findings. The method of synthesising the data depends on the nature of the data. Broadly speaking, there are two different methods of synthesising data in a systematic review: statistical meta-analysis or a narrative synthesis. A single systematic review could use both approaches, and there are benefits of this, but usually a reviewer will apply one or the other.

2.4.1 How do I conduct a narrative synthesis?

When a statistical meta-analysis is not warranted (in the situation when studies are not sufficiently homogenous (see Section 2.4.2)), or when qualitative data is to be synthesised or not desired, the alternative is to conduct a narrative synthesis.

It is important to remember that a narrative synthesis is a synthesis and not a lengthy description of each study included in the review. It is recommended that you spend some time considering the structure of your synthesis after you are familiar with all the studies included in your review, to ensure that the synthesis is presented in such a way that the main points of interest are highlighted rather than lost in a mire of information.

It is normally the case that you will want to present summary tables in a narrative synthesis. These tables can be used to summarise the main characteristics of each study included in the review. This will give the reader an overview of the types of research included and will avoid the need for a lengthy textual description of each study. Indeed, it is useful to provide a summary description of individual studies before synthesising them. It might be pertinent to divide the studies in your review into meaningful subgroups (perhaps created on the basis of study quality) and present a summary table for each subgroup of studies. You might even wish to present a synthesis of your data divided by these subgroups, with a few final paragraphs drawing together the information from each subgroup analysis.

Unlike statistical meta-analysis, there are no 'rules' for a narrative synthesis. The format of a narrative synthesis varies to a much greater extent than the format of a statistical meta-analysis. This is entirely appropriate as a narrative synthesis is a way of summarising a range of quantitative findings from a variety of study designs, or a method for summarising qualitative findings or a method for integrating qualitative and quantitative results. This flexibility is the strength of narrative synthesis. Nevertheless, I realise that this information may not be particularly helpful for trainee psychologists who are undertaking a systematic review and who want to have some idea about how a narrative synthesis should be conducted. So, although no 'rules' exist, some guidelines might be useful. Some detailed guidelines for structuring a narrative synthesis are provided by Popay et al. (2006). Here, I have tried to summarise some of the main points.

In general, there are three key elements in a narrative synthesis: conducting a preliminary synthesis, exploring relationships in the data and assessing the robustness of the synthesis outcomes. A preliminary synthesis is a synthesis of the key findings of the studies included in the review which is organised in such a way that it will lend itself to insights into the reasons for any heterogeneity across study findings. In other words, you cannot conduct a preliminary synthesis without knowing what messages you want to deliver in the narrative synthesis as a whole, because the preliminary synthesis presents information to the reader in a structured way which facilitates future comparisons in the narrative synthesis.

Exploring the relationships in the data is a method of narratively exploring the heterogeneity in study findings uncovered in the preliminary synthesis. Therefore, you need to examine patterns of findings within the data and what can help to explain these patterns. For example, can we explain similarities and differences in study findings on the basis of study quality, study location, when the study was conducted, the type of sample and so on. This element of the narrative synthesis represents a departure from description and a move towards integration of findings.

Assessing the robustness of the synthesis refers to a critique of the extent to which the conclusions posited by the systematic review are affected by the methodological quality of the research included in the systematic review and by the techniques of the review itself. In effect, this part of the narrative synthesis indicates the limitations of the conclusions of the review and why those limitations have arisen. This element of a narrative synthesis is important in terms of informing future research and/or informing practice. In a sense, it is your attempt to help the reader interpret your synthesis in a reasonable manner. Of course, this element is equally important in a statistical meta-analysis.

2.4.1.1 Synthesising qualitative research

Although the guidelines referred to here were written primarily for a narrative synthesis of quantitative research, the principles could also apply to a narrative synthesis of qualitative research. However, as qualitative research is based on a different epistemological approach than quantitative research, the synthesis of qualitative research raises further issues for consideration which are worthy of highlighting.

Qualitative research tends to support the generation of data at the idiographic level, emphasising the importance of the richness in the depth of information obtained from individuals and highlighting the value of this type of research as opposed to the statistical approach of summarising groups into single statistics with an obsession on the representativeness of this summary statistic (which is often not demonstrably achieved). Not surprisingly, then, the notion of reducing and synthesising the findings of qualitative research in the context of a systematic review is an anathema to many qualitative researchers. In addition, proposing a synthesis of qualitative findings suggests that qualitative research is a single entity. Quantitative research can take many forms but tends to stem from very similar theoretical traditions. Qualitative research, on the other hand, stems from a variety of different and often opposing theoretical traditions, and so a synthesis of qualitative data is not comparing like with like.

However, qualitative research does not exist in isolation, and qualitative researchers are affected by previous research in their area. Therefore, at some level, a synthesis of qualitative research takes place, although sometimes not in an explicit manner, and is necessary for qualitative research to make ongoing contributions to our knowledge in the area. It is likely that in the past qualitative researchers have been resistant to the notion of synthesising qualitative data because the methods proposed often involved the reduction of the qualitative findings to a quantitative score to facilitate a synthesis! However, more recently, genuine attempts have been made to develop appropriate methods for conducting a synthesis of qualitative data while maintaining the richness of the information provided. Consequently, the debate about the synthesis of qualitative research is shifting away from whether it should take place to how it can be facilitated in an acceptable way.

One of the most promising methods developed to guide the synthesis of qualitative research is the concept of meta-ethnography (Noblit & Hare, 1988). Meta-ethnography is not a way of summarising findings into an aggregate but of relating findings from different studies to one another, using an interpretative approach. Meta-ethnography is, therefore, a method of synthesising qualitative research which is not at odds with the epistemological approach which drives qualitative research. Noblit and Hare (1988) suggest seven steps in a meta-ethnography, which are further discussed by Atkins et al. (2008):

1. *Getting started* – determine an appropriate review question that can be answered by qualitative research.
2. *Deciding what is relevant to the initial interest.* This step is similar to the process of defining the review protocol outlined in Sections 2.2.3 and 2.2.4 for quantitative research. In other words, you need to define the focus of the review (the eligibility criteria), the quality criteria and how these will be assessed and the search strategy. This step also encompasses the process of retrieving the articles and applying the eligibility and quality assessment criteria. Therefore, by the end

of this step, you should have identified a relevant pool of articles for inclusion in the review.

3. *Reading the studies.* This refers to the process of becoming familiar with the studies and extracting the relevant data. Some of this data will be descriptive information about the sample, context and so on, but it will also include themes and interpretations made by each study's authors.

4. *Determine how the studies are related.* This can be done by organising the themes/interpretations into categories of information. However, it is likely that these categories, and their content, will need to be reviewed and revised during this process and that the creation of categories will require some critical reflection.

5. *Translating studies into one another.* This refers to the comparisons made among the themes/interpretations presented in each study. There is no set method of making these comparisons. It might be useful to proceed through the studies in chronological order to get a sense of the development of the topic, or it might be useful to create subcategories of studies which have a slightly different focus on the review question.

6. *Synthesising translations.* In a sense, this is similar to the process of moving from emerging themes to a higher-order interpretation that exists in a primary qualitative research study. It is the process of trying to make sense of the entirety of the information presented.

7. *Expressing the synthesis.* Disseminating the findings of the review in a manner that is accessible and representative of the complexity of the information reviewed. Anyone who has ever written a research paper based on qualitative data will understand the difficulty of matching these two, often opposing, aims.

Usefully, most health and clinical psychology trainees in the UK have a relatively good understanding of the basics of statistical analysis, which allows books like this one to be written without devoting a great deal of space to explaining these basics. Sadly, the same cannot be said of trainees' knowledge of qualitative research. The undergraduate training of psychologists in the UK is still driven by a positivist, experimental approach, and, as a result, it is not possible to discuss meta-ethnography further in a brief and clear way in this book which would do justice to the method. I can only recommend the original text of Noblit and Hare (1988), an example of a comprehensive systematic review which incorporates a meta-ethnography (Hefferon, Grealy & Mutrie, 2009), and a worked example of a meta-ethnography of lay meanings of medicine (Britten et al., 2002).

2.4.2 When is it appropriate to conduct a statistical meta-analysis?

A statistical meta-analysis is a method of reducing the relevant data extracted from the articles in the review to a statistic which summarises the results across the articles. Conducting a statistical meta-analysis rather than a narrative synthesis of the data requires a good working knowledge of statistics, and often the help of a statistician is required here. However, a statistical meta-analysis can provide a concise and powerful summary of data extracted from research and will directly address the review question of interest. Therefore, where a statistical meta-analysis is possible, it is to be encouraged. Yet, systematic reviews conducted in the areas of health psychology and clinical psychology often do not lend themselves to the calculation of a statistical meta-analysis.

Basically, meta-analysis is appropriate when the key pieces of quantitative data extracted from the articles are similar enough (or sufficiently homogenous) to be combined in a summary statistic. The key pieces of data here refer to things like the nature of the intervention (if one is included), the quantitative measures used in the research and the study design. But how homogenous must the studies be before they can be considered sufficiently homogenous? This is an important decision that must be made by the review team and will be based on the nature of the review question and the usefulness to psychologists of any answers obtained by statistical meta-analysis. Let's look at an example to highlight the issues that need to be considered in this decision.

Consider a systematic review which addresses a question of effectiveness (this is a type of review question which most often lends itself to a statistical meta-analysis). We have seen an example of such a question in an earlier section: 'when used among adults with a diagnosis of depression who have been referred to an adult mental health service, is mindfulness-based cognitive therapy more effective at reducing levels of self-reported depression than bibliotherapy?'

With this review question in mind, we would probably review a group of relevant studies which were apparently homogenous, that is, the studies would all include adults with a confirmed diagnosis of depression attending an adult mental health service, the intervention group would always receive mindfulness-based cognitive therapy (MBCT), the comparison group would always receive bibliotherapy and the outcomes measured would always include an assessment of levels of self-reported depression. At first glance, it seems that the data extracted from these studies is likely to be similar enough to warrant a statistical meta-analysis. This may be the case, but here are some examples of the issues that the review team needs to consider before deciding that the extracted data is sufficiently homogenous for a meta-analysis:

- Is the outcome measure (depression) assessed in the same way? In other words, do all the studies use the same questionnaire to assess levels of depression, and, if not, can the scores from the different measures be transformed in such a way to make them directly comparable?
- Is the diagnosis of depression provided in a standardised way by similar individuals? For example, in some studies the 'diagnosis' of depression may be assigned by a mental health nurse when the participants reach a certain cut-off score on a self-report questionnaire. In other studies, the 'diagnosis' of depression may be assigned after the participant has engaged in a structured clinical interview with a psychiatrist. Are these 'diagnoses' sufficiently similar for the review team to be satisfied that the participants in the different studies should be combined into a single group for the purposes of statistical meta-analysis?
- Is the intervention provided at the individual or group level, and, consequently, are the results from these different interventions sufficiently similar to be combined?
- Is the type of bibliotherapy sufficiently similar across studies, or is one type of bibliotherapy likely to be more effective than another?
- Is it appropriate to combine the results obtained from different study designs? For example, should the results obtained from a randomised controlled trial be combined with results obtained from a non-randomised controlled trial?

Clearly, there are issues specific to each systematic review which need to be considered before a statistical meta-analysis is undertaken, and it is not always easy to reach a consensus within a review team about which data should be included in a statistical meta-analysis. Helpfully, when consensus cannot be reached, there is a potential solution – sensitivity analysis. Sensitivity analysis is a way of determining whether the conclusions of the meta-analysis would be altered if certain data were omitted/included in the meta-analysis. For example, imagine that the review team cannot reach consensus on the final bullet point above. In other words, some members of the team feel that it is OK to combine the findings from the randomised and non-randomised controlled trials, but other members of the team feel strongly that this is not comparing like with like. The potential solution here is to conduct a meta-analysis with both types of study design included and then to conduct the meta-analysis with the non-randomised controlled trials excluded. If the two meta-analyses result in the same conclusions, then we can conclude that including the non-randomised controlled trials in the meta-analysis has no important effect, and, therefore, this is acceptable.

Nevertheless, it is important to be aware that sensitivity analysis results in an increase in the amount of statistical analyses conducted, and it in no way replaces sound decisions based on conceptual issues. Sensitivity analyses might also highlight a lack of homogeneity in studies that requires some explanation. Section 2.4.3 includes a further discussion about the exploration of homogeneity and heterogeneity in statistical meta-analysis.

2.4.3   How do I conduct a statistical meta-analysis?

The basic principle behind statistical meta-analysis is to convert the relevant data obtained from the reviewed articles into a standard version of the data, to allow them to be combined. The conversion of the data obtained into a standard version of the data usually takes the form of creating an effect size. A pooled effect size is then calculated to represent the combined results across all the studies reviewed. Let's look at each of these two steps in turn.

2.4.3.1   Calculating an effect size

An effect size is a statistic which summarises outcome data from a single study in a standard way to allow comparisons to be made with results from other studies. Essentially, it is a method of converting raw scores to a standardised scale. The effect size which is most useful for you to calculate will depend on the type of data you have available, which is in turn dictated by the review question and the types of study design included in your review. The effect sizes most commonly used in meta-analysis are those that relate to differences between two groups or relationships between two variables. For example:

- When the effect of interest is the difference between the means of two groups (for example, an intervention group and a control group), you can summarise this information using an effect size such as Cohen's d. Cohen's d is calculated by subtracting the mean score for group 1 from the mean score for group 2 and then dividing the result by the common standard deviation for the two groups ((mean2–mean1) / standard deviation). The common standard deviation is the standard deviation statistic that is shared by both groups. In practice, the standard deviation for both groups in this type of study is unlikely to be exactly the same, but it should be similar. Therefore, the average standard deviation of the two groups can be used as the common standard deviation. In this way, Cohen's d provides an indication of the extent to which the two groups differ – the size of the difference or size of the effect. The difference between the two groups is expressed in terms of standard deviations. For example, a Cohen's d of 0.5 means that the two groups differ by 0.5 of a standard deviation.

- When the effect of interest is the difference between proportions of two groups (for example, the difference between two groups on a dichotomous outcome measure such as anxious vs not anxious), a useful effect size is the odds ratio.
- When the effect of interest is the relationship between two continuous variables (for example, the relationship between a measure of hopelessness and time spent studying psychology), a useful effect size is the correlation coefficient (r).

Box 2.2 Converting between effect sizes

To convert Cohen's d to r,

$$r = \frac{d}{\sqrt{d^2 + \frac{(N^2 - 2N)}{n_1 n_2}}}$$

where n_1 = sample size in group 1; n_2 = sample size in group 2; $N = n_1 + n_2$

To convert r to Cohen's d,

$$d = \frac{2r}{\sqrt{1 - r^2}}$$

In practice, it doesn't matter which of the effect sizes mentioned that you choose to use, because it is possible to convert one effect size into another (see Box 2.2 for an example). The purpose of listing different effect sizes here according to study design is to highlight the types of effect size that will probably be easiest for you to obtain, depending on the type of study designs you have. The important thing is that you end up with an effect size of the same format for all of the data that you want to include in your meta-analysis.

Finally, in this section, I would like to deal with a common question from trainees engaged in meta-analysis to assess the effect of an intervention. In these cases, you are reviewing studies with some type of experimental design, and, usually, you are interested in the differences between two groups (an intervention group and a comparison group). This leads you to calculate Cohen's d as the effect size. However, often you are presented with pre-test and post-test data for each group (at least you should be), so you are left wondering whether you should use the post-test means and standard deviations to calculate the effect size between groups or whether you should use the difference between the pre-test and post-test means for each group to calculate the effect size between groups. The second option appears to be the most useful because it focuses on a comparison of the size of the change in each group, yet in published meta-analyses the post-test scores are often used. The argument for using post-test scores is that if you wish to use change scores for the calculation of your effect size, then you will need the standard deviations of the change scores, and these are not always reported. However, Morris (2008) provides a comparison of different methods of estimating an effect size for difference scores based on the pre-test and post-test summary statistics, and where the standard deviation of the change scores is not required. Box 2.3 presents the formula for the effect size which Morris proposes as the best of the effect sizes he compared. This effect size is based on the formula for an effect size similar to Cohen's d known as Hedge's g, and it provides an unbiased estimate of the population effect size with a known sampling variance. Yet it is important to note that this effect size may underestimate the true sampling variance. In practice, this means that a meta-analysis based on this effect size is likely to demonstrate heterogeneity across effect sizes even when no heterogeneity truly exists (see the next section for a discussion of heterogeneity in meta-analyses).

Box 2.3   An effect size for pre-test–post-test comparisons between groups

Effect size=

$$c \left[\frac{\text{(Difference between pretest and posttest means for group 1)} - \text{(Difference between pretest and posttest means for group 2)}}{SD_{pre}} \right]$$

where $SD_{pre} = \sqrt{\frac{(n_1-1)SD_{1pre}^2 + (n_2-1)SD_{2pre}^2}{n_1+n_2-2}}$ and $c = 1 - \frac{3}{4(n_1+n_2-2)-1}$

where n_1 = sample size in group 1, n_2 = sample size in group 2 SD_{1pre} = SD for the pre-test scores in group 1, SD_{2pre} = SD for the pre-test scores in group 2.

2.4.3.2   Pooling effect sizes

The second step in a statistical meta-analysis is to combine the effect sizes for each research study into an overall effect size which represents the average effect across the studies. You might think that the simple thing to do here would be to work out the mean effect size for the studies in your review (that is, sum the effect size from each study and divide by the number of studies). In principle, this is what we want to do, but we need to take account of the differences among the studies as we are calculating this average. For example, it may be that some of your effect sizes have been derived from studies with very large sample sizes, and other effect sizes have been derived from studies with very small sample sizes. It would be inappropriate to simply take the mean of these effect sizes without taking account of the sample size from which they were derived. Primarily, this is inappropriate because (with all else being held constant), the larger the sample size, the smaller the standard error. So larger sample sizes enable us to be more confident about our findings. To address this issue, effect sizes are weighted by a factor that is based on the sample size from which they were derived. After the weighting factor has been applied, the mean weighted effect size and confidence intervals for this average weighted effect size can be calculated.

There are different methods of calculating weighting factors (including weighting factors based on a quality score for a study rather than sample size) and different methods for calculating significance levels and/ or confidence intervals associated with the average weighted effect size (see Field, 2001 for a discussion and comparison of different methods of combining effect sizes). Rather than enter into a detailed discussion about these issues, I have provided a brief summary.

It is generally accepted that the most appropriate weighting factor for effect sizes is a weighting factor based on sample sizes. The weighting factor to be used will depend on the effect size used. After each effect size has been multiplied by its appropriate weighting factor, the method chosen for combining the weighted effect sizes primarily depends on whether you are conducting a fixed or random effects analysis. Box 2.4 provides examples of calculating an average weighted effect size assuming a fixed effects model.

Box 2.4   Average weighted effect sizes (assuming fixed effects)

When using a correlation coefficient (r) as the effect size, often the first step is to convert each r to Z using Fisher's transformation:

$$Z_r = \frac{1}{2}\ln\left(\frac{1+r}{1-r}\right)$$

Box 2.4   Continued

In this case, it has been shown (Hedges & Olkin, 1985) that the optimal weight for Z_r is n−3, where n is the sample size from which the correlation coefficient was obtained. Therefore, when using correlation coefficients, the weighted effect size is given by: $(n-3)Z_r$.

When using Cohen's d as the effect size the weighting factor (W) for each effect size is given by:

$$W = \frac{2(n_1 + n_2)m_1n_2}{2(n_1 + n_2)^2 + n_1n_2d^2}$$

where n_1 = sample size in group 1, n_2 = sample size in group 2

Therefore, when using Cohen's d, the weighted effect size is given by W(d).

Regardless of which effect size measure is used, the average weighted effect size across studies is the sum of the weighted effect sizes for each study divided by the sum of the weights. A 95 % confidence interval around this average weighted effect size can then be calculated using the following formula:

$$\text{average weighted effect size} \pm 1.96\sqrt{\text{inverse of the sum of the weights}}$$

A fixed effects analysis differs from a random effects analysis in terms of the assumptions made about the effect size. A fixed effects analysis assumes that there is a single effect size in the population which all the studies are trying to estimate. A random effects analysis assumes that the studies in your review are estimating effect sizes which differ from study to study. In other words, a random effects analysis assumes that the effect sizes obtained from the different studies in your review will vary not only because of sampling error (as the fixed effects model assumes) but also for other reasons. Basically, this means that when you use a fixed effects model, the inferences you make really extend only to the studies included in your review, whereas with a random effects model you are permitting an extension of your inferences to similar studies in the area not included in your review. The distinction is important because different results will be obtained depending on which model you use. However, where the studies included in your meta-analysis are homogenous, the results of a random and fixed effects analysis will be identical.

2.4.3.2 (a)   Exploring heterogeneity

On the basis that you have considered carefully the conceptual reasons for combining studies in a statistical meta-analysis, to ensure that the studies are sufficiently homogenous (see Section 2.4.2), it is still possible (in fact, very likely) that heterogeneity will be present in your analysis because of differences in the studies' findings. The question is whether the heterogeneity found in your meta-analysis is greater than would be expected by chance. If it is, then it is important to identify the likely source(s) of this heterogeneity and address it in your analysis.

Statistically, the presence of significant heterogeneity in your meta-analysis can be investigated using the Q statistic. The Q statistic is an indication of the extent to which each effect size in the meta-analysis differs from the average effect size. The larger the Q statistic, the greater the heterogeneity in your meta-analysis. The statistical significance of the Q statistic can be determined by reference to the chi-square distribution with n–1 degrees of freedom, where n is the total number of studies in your meta-analysis. However, the Q statistic is not a powerful statistic. In other words, it will not detect statistically significant heterogeneity when there are a small number of studies in the meta-analysis (as will likely be the case in your systematic review). Consequently, another statistic (I^2) is recommended. I^2 is a measure of the extent of inconsistency between studies. It is expressed as a percentage, with an I^2 of 0 % meaning that none of the variations across studies is due to heterogeneity rather than chance (all the variance is due to sampling error within studies). I^2 is calculated by subtracting the degrees of freedom from Q and then dividing the answer by Q. The result is then multiplied by 100 to allow expression as a percentage. Both Q and I^2 are calculated by most software packages designed to perform meta-analysis.

2.3.4.2 (b)   Forest plots

As with all statistics, graphical methods are a useful addition to help provide further understanding of the nature of the data. In meta-analysis, a forest plot is often used to display the weighted effect sizes for each study included in the meta-analysis and the average weighted effect size. This plot is a very useful method of exploring the nature of any heterogeneity discovered in the statistical summary and may help you to determine the best method of dealing with heterogeneity.

An example of a forest plot is provided in Figure 2.1. The plot is a fictional one and relates to a meta-analysis conducted as part of a systematic review to address the question: 'when used among adults with a diagnosis of depression who have been referred to an adult mental health service, is mindfulness-based cognitive therapy more effective at reducing

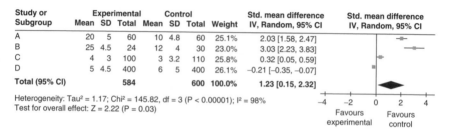

Study or Subgroup	Experimental			Control			Weight	Std. mean difference IV, Random, 95% CI	Std. mean difference IV, Random, 95% CI
	Mean	SD	Total	Mean	SD	Total			
A	20	5	60	10	4.8	60	25.1%	2.03 [1.58, 2.47]	
B	25	4.5	24	12	4	30	23.0%	3.03 [2.23, 3.83]	
C	4	3	100	3	3.2	110	25.8%	0.32 [0.05, 0.59]	
D	5	4.5	400	6	5	400	26.1%	−0.21 [−0.35, −0.07]	
Total (95% CI)			584			600	100.0%	1.23 [0.15, 2.32]	

Heterogeneity: Tau² = 1.17; Chi² = 145.82, df = 3 (P < 0.00001); I² = 98%
Test for overall effect: Z = 2.22 (P = 0.03)

Figure 2.1 Forest Plot for a review of intervention studies (generated by RevMan 5)

levels of self-reported depression than bibliotherapy?' In the forest plot, the location of the effect size for each study is indicated by a box (and the size of the box indicates the weighting given to the effect size), with the confidence intervals on either side of this effect size represented by the lines extending to either side of each box. The midpoint of the diamond represents the average weighted effect size, with the points of the diamond on the left and the right stretching out to the confidence limits.

The statistics relating to this plot are Q = 145.82, df = 3, p < 0.001, I² = 98 %. Clearly, a substantial proportion of the variance is due to heterogeneity, and the plot provides some clues about the location of this heterogeneity. It is clear from the plot that the effect sizes for studies A and B are similar and that the effect sizes for studies C and D are similar, but the effect sizes of A and B are different from the effect sizes of C and D. To understand this heterogeneity, we will need to examine the characteristics of these studies. We need to determine whether studies A and B have something in common which is different from studies C and D. The difference may be, for example, that studies A and B have been conducted in a different country than studies C and D, or studies A and B use a different design than studies C and D. In that case, we might want to present separate meta-analyses for these two subgroups of studies. However, conducting further subgroup analyses such as this reduces the power in your meta-analysis.

2.3.4.2 (c)   Publication bias

Publication bias refers to the bias that is potentially present in your review because you have included only published studies. Published studies are likely to be biased for a number of reasons, one of which is the file drawer problem. This refers to the possibility that there are studies which have been conducted by researchers but which did not show positive (non-significant) results, and, therefore, have remained in the researcher's file drawer rather than being published. Another example of publication bias is where a study is either less likely to be published or less likely to be included in a review because it is not written in English.

Publication bias can be avoided, to some extent, by ensuring that your search strategy covers grey literature and involves contact with known researchers in the field. However, there is also a train of thought which suggests that publication bias usually omits small, poor quality studies (which is the reason why they are not published or submitted for publication), so going to extremes to find these studies is not only a waste of resources but also can introduce bias towards small, poor quality studies into your review (Egger, Jüni, Bartlett, Holenstein & Sterne, 2003).

Various methods have been developed for detecting and dealing with potential publication bias in systematic reviews, such as funnel plots and the trim and fill method (Duval & Tweedie, 2000) and fail safe n (Rosenthal, 1979). However, they are not uncontroversial (e.g. Evans, 1996; Lau, Ioannidis, Terrin, Schmid & Olkin, 2006; Peters, Sutton, Jones, Abrams & Rushton, 2007).

2.4.4 Where should I disseminate the systematic review findings?

Like any research where resources have been invested, there is an onus on the authors to at least attempt to disseminate the findings in an appropriate forum. As a trainee psychologist following a programme towards qualification as a clinical or health psychologist, you will undoubtedly be expected to present your review in some form of written report for assessment. However, the purpose of conducting any research (or at least research conducted at postgraduate level and beyond) is to further knowledge in the area, and this aim will be achieved only if the findings of the research are disseminated among the likely users of this information. The recognition of this and the action taken to achieve this goal speaks of the professional competence of psychologists.

Furthermore, it is important to remember that other people have probably contributed time and other resources to the completion of this review, and it might be the case that they will need to justify this investment in terms of outcomes. These outcomes are usually evidenced by peer-reviewed publications.

Therefore, I would encourage you to consider producing your systematic review in a format suitable for publication in an appropriate peer-reviewed journal. There are many journals in the field of health and clinical psychology and journals specific to the disease/condition of interest to the research which will publish both primary research and systematic reviews. Your supervisor will probably be the best source of information regarding an appropriate journal for your review. At the time of writing, there are two journals which focus solely on publishing reviews in the areas of health or clinical psychology, which may be relevant to you: 'Clinical Psychology Review' and 'Health Psychology Review'. Both these journals are not only potential outlets for the publication of your review but also are useful journals to browse to examine how different types of reviews (both systematic and traditional comprehensive literature reviews) are presented.

It may be that the format of the presentation of your systematic review is dictated by your supervisor or your course regulations. Whether this is the case or not, the journal to which you propose to submit your review will have its own specific guidelines for the presentation of your manuscript, so you should make yourself aware of these. Many of these journals (particularly those from the medical field) will suggest that you follow a standard set of guidelines for the presentation of systematic reviews of quantitative research. These guidelines provide a useful template for structuring reviews. There are two standard guidelines: PRISMA and MOOSE.

PRISMA refers to the Preferred Reporting Items for Systematic Reviews and Meta-Analysis (Moher et al., 2009). It is an updated version of the QUOROM statement (Moher et al., 1999). Further information about PRISMA can be found at http://www.prisma-statement.org/index.htm. MOOSE refers to Meta-Analysis of Observational Studies in Epidemiology (Stroup et al., 2000). The PRISMA statement is based on conducting systematic reviews of randomised controlled trials, although they have moved away from a sole focus on randomised controlled trials (as was the case in the QUORUM statement) to guidelines that apply, more generally, to reviews of intervention studies.

Summary of the Systematic Review Process

Identify the need for a review

Specify the review question

Write a review protocol – contains background and rationale for the review, the review question, planned search strategy, eligibility and quality criteria, and the plan for data extraction, analysis and dissemination

Conduct literature search

Assess eligibility of retrieved articles

Extract relevant data from relevant articles

Assess quality of relevant articles

Synthesise data

Disseminate a report of the review

Further reading

NHS Centre for Reviews and Dissemination Guidance for Undertaking Reviews in Health Care. Available at: http://www.york.ac.uk/inst/crd/index_guidance.htm

Petticrew, M. & Roberts, H. (2006). *Systematic Reviews in the Social Sciences: A Practical Guide*. Oxford: Blackwell.

UK Cochrane Centre online learning materials. Available at: http://www.cochrane.co.uk/en/newPage3.html

3

Developing a Research Proposal

● ●

All clinical/health psychology trainees are required to conduct an empirical research project as part of the requirements to demonstrate research competence. Consequently, you will need to formulate a research proposal, which is often formally assessed as evidence towards research competence. This chapter will address the topics that clinical/health psychology trainees often struggle with when formulating a research proposal. It will begin by discussing how a research question develops, taking into consideration the practical and philosophical issues that need to be considered when a research proposal is developed. The chapter will then outline the different types of research design that could be considered to address a research question, including ethical issues associated with these research designs.

3.1 Developing a research idea

The research project that we will look at in this and the following chapters is known by different names in different training programmes. It may be called, for example, the major research project, the large scale research project, the empirical research project, the research thesis. Whatever the label, the research project is defined by the quality of the research that is expected. Sometimes the labels used can be misleading – for example, 'large scale research project' or 'major research project' might suggest that the defining property is the size of the sample; 'empirical research project' might lead a trainee to believe that the emphasis is on quantitative research. These misconceptions can sometimes result in trainees failing to focus on the important aspects of the research project – that it is research conducted in a rigorous manner, which advances our knowledge in the area of interest. The findings of the research project should have important implications for clinical/health psychology researchers and/or practitioners, and (as a result of these qualities) the research should be publishable in a peer-reviewed journal. These criteria can sound quite daunting if you have never completed a research project of this type before (and the vast majority of clinical/health psychology trainees that I have met over the years fall into this category), and you may well be wondering where to start. The answer is to start with a good research question. If you develop an appropriate and feasible research question, then everything else will follow from this.

3.1.1 How do I identify a research idea?

The answer here may be easier than it first appears. Supervisors and staff involved in clinical and health psychology training programmes are very aware of the time constraints under which your training takes place, and most will acknowledge that many trainees do not have the time to develop a research project from scratch and complete it to an appropriate standard before the clock runs out on their training. Therefore, training programmes will often provide some direction to trainees about the types of research project that they can undertake. The extent of this direction will, of course, vary. Some programmes will provide a list of general topics in which research projects could be facilitated; some programmes will invite internal and external psychologists to present research projects (at the initial stage of development) to trainees and allow the trainees to choose which they become involved with; and some programmes will be more prescriptive about the specific research projects that trainees can undertake. These variations are dependent on the resources available to the programmes and the external constraints under which the programme operates. Whatever the style of the programme on which you are enrolled in, it is important to remember that it is you who will ultimately need to defend your research project in a viva and/or in a project report, so you need to be centrally involved in all aspects of the research process, including the development of the question. In other words, just because someone else gives you a research question or directs you towards one, it does not mean that this is a good question – you need to satisfy yourself that it is. Additionally, I know of many health/clinical psychology trainees who have developed their research question and have been able to complete a very high quality research project on time, so don't rule out this possibility.

My advice to all trainees (in fact to anyone undertaking a research project) is to choose a research project which interests you. Conducting your research project will be a time-consuming process which will require you to troubleshoot, problem solve, and develop good coping strategies and a high level of perseverance – all very valuable skills in your working life. But, as a result, for some trainees what begins as something interesting can often become something frustrating. Think how much worse this will be if you begin with something which is not really interesting! Of course, being interested in a topic may be necessary, but it is not sufficient to justify a good research idea.

Good research ideas emanate from a number of different sources. Broadly speaking, research ideas emanate either from theory or from clinical experience, or from both. Firstly, research questions can be generated to address identified gaps in the area of research. An excellent source for identifying gaps in an area of research is a good quality literature review (such as a systematic review). Good quality published reviews will draw together known information in an area and indicate what remains to be known, thereby providing a good rationale for a research idea, on the basis that no further relevant research has been published since the review was undertaken. Indeed, recent primary research in an area will often provide something similar, in a more limited way, so carefully reading the discussions of research papers published in your area of interest will be useful. Secondly, case studies, or the clinical experience of psychologists and other health professionals will identify issues of clinical interest which require further research. Given that a good research project will tackle questions of relevance to psychologists, discussing your area of interest with a psychologist might be a good method of generating a research idea.

What should become clear is that the development of a research idea is a process rather than an event. In other words, the development of a research idea is not something you decide to do during a free slot in your timetable. Rather it is something which will evolve over time by becoming familiar with the existing research literature in an area, particularly the most recent research; listening to psychologists who know the area; and discussing the idea with others, including your peers. It is never too early to begin this process.

3.1.2 Is my research idea feasible?

Determining the feasibility of your research idea is a process which involves moving from an idea to a specific, concrete question and thinking through the practicalities of the idea. For example, you might have an interest in examining the psychological benefits of outdoor organised physical activity. By considering the practicalities of doing research in this area (such as what types of psychological variables are likely to be affected by outdoor physical activity and what types of physical activity should be considered), you can begin to convert this idea into a more specific question, such as: 'is there any difference between those who engage in regular exercise as a result of conservation activities and those who engage in regular exercise by attending an indoor gym, in terms of their self-esteem levels and perceptions of social support?' This question will need to be operationalised further (see Section 3.2.2), but you have started the process of moving from a research idea to a research question, and this will help you to determine the feasibility of your idea. Some of the feasibility issues cannot be fully addressed until the research proposal is being completed, and you know exactly what you intend to do, but there are some issues that can be considered at an early stage to determine whether the research idea is likely to be feasible and therefore justify the effort required to develop a full proposal.

What follow are questions that need to be considered when determining the feasibility of your research idea. I strongly encourage you to re-examine this list after you have developed a full research proposal, as a way of assessing your proposal.

Does the research have a sound rationale? You should clarify that the research is needed, that it addresses a gap in the existing research. One of the most effective ways of testing your rationale is to present it verbally to others. Sometimes we can justify a proposed course of research in our head, but it is only when we need to clarify and justify the research to someone else that we realise where the holes in our logic exist. It is worth presenting your rationale to people who know little or nothing about the area, to ensure that it makes sense to them, and to present your rationale to people who know the area, to ensure that you are not proposing a research project which is naïve in its design.

Is the research suitable? You need to consider whether the proposed research meets the specific requirements of the programme on which you are enrolled. The chief consideration here is likely to be the availability of an appropriate supervisor willing to supervise the area of research and the type of methodology involved.

Do you have sufficient resources to complete the research? All research needs to be resourced in some form or other. At the very least, one key resource will be the amount of time you have available. There is no point in developing an excellent research idea which is impossible to deliver in the time available to you. It is likely that your proposed research project will also require some financial investment. For example, you may need to purchase psychological tests or questionnaires, or you may need to conduct interviews with participants and will need travelling expenses for either you or the participants. It is important that you check whether such resources are available to you.

Is there anything in the research that is outside your control? Are you relying on anyone else? There may be elements of the proposed research which are crucial to its success but which are not under your control. You should try to make a realistic assessment of these risks and any solutions to problems that may arise. For example, you might be interested in the quality of life of people with schizophrenia and whether this is influenced by the presence of childhood trauma. Your idea is to sample a group of people with schizophrenia from an outpatients' clinic and assess childhood trauma and quality of life to determine the relationship between these variables. Here there is a potential risk to the research of finding that only a few people in your sample report any type of childhood trauma (despite previous literature suggesting that this would be unlikely). This will make it very difficult, if not impossible, to address your question of interest. Therefore, before engaging in this research you would want to reassure yourself about the prevalence of childhood trauma within the population you have access to and/or widen the research aim to include secondary research questions to be addressed as a 'fall-back' plan.

One of the things that might be outside your control is the behaviour of others who are crucial to the success of the research. For example, your proposed research may rely on other health professionals (other psychologists, medics, nurses, for example) to identify potential participants for your research and perhaps even obtain consent from potential participants for you to contact them. The likelihood of these arrangements being successful will depend on how committed these people are to assisting you with your research and how realistic they are about the amount of their time this will take. In these situations, I cannot emphasise strongly enough the importance of ensuring that these crucial people are fully signed up (in at least a metaphorical sense) to your proposed research project (see Chapter 1 for a discussion of negotiating collaborative relationships).

Is the population difficult to access? Perhaps you have a very good research idea, but it requires access to a population of which there is a limited number in your vicinity. Will it be easy to extend your recruitment outside the local area, in the time you have available? Additionally, your population may be transient, which can cause difficulties for research with a longitudinal design. For example, you might wish to evaluate the effect of an intervention for a group of inpatients. The evaluation will require at least a pre-test and a post-test, with the intervention delivered in the interim. If the intervention takes four weeks and the average length of hospital stay is four weeks, then organising the pre-test and post-test could be difficult.

Will the outcomes of the research project inform psychological theory/practice? The level of competence in research required from a clinical or health psychologist is that you can produce research which adds to our knowledge in the area. In other words, this is not simply an exercise in doing research; it is not sufficient to demonstrate that you know something about the different elements of a research project. Rather it is necessary that you demonstrate, through your research project, that you can contribute meaningfully to psychological knowledge.

Have you developed a question on the basis of a sound rationale or have you decided on a methodology which you have tried to fit a question to? If your research question has a sound rationale, then it is a good research question. Your next step is to develop an appropriate method of answering the research question and determine whether the proposed research is feasible. Unfortunately, I have encountered many trainees who have decided that they want to use a particular research method and then try to develop a research question to suit this method. For example, when I ask trainees whether they have found an idea for their research project, some of them will say something like 'No, but I want to do something qualitative'. Their reason for this could be based in some entrenched epistemological stance, which would make it understandable to some extent, but usually it is because they 'don't really like statistics'. In my head, this is translated into 'I just want to get a project done with as little bother for me as possible – I don't really want to be challenged by it'. While I can understand the desire to expedite the process in light of other demands on your time, more often than not, this approach results in an ill-specified research question with a questionable rationale. Good research *requires* challenges to be met and dealt with, and if you try to take shortcuts and/or avoid challenges in the research project, this will most likely result in a sub-standard final written report and/or in your performance in the viva, and it will be obvious to your assessor.

The outcomes of these considerations should then be formalised and written in the format of a research proposal, which will enable others to provide feedback on your considerations and perhaps identify additional issues that need to be addressed before the research proceeds.

3.2 Content of the research proposal

Good quality research is more likely to result from a well-considered proposal. Time invested in the development of the proposal is time which will be saved when the research is underway. This section intends to provide a guide for the type of information that should be presented in the proposal. Although different training programmes may have different requirements for the formulation of your research proposal, most research proposals will contain a title of the proposed research, a discussion of the background to and rationale for the proposed research, a statement of the aims of the proposed research, a research protocol (plan for the conduct of the research), data analysis plans, dissemination plans, research governance and ethics processes, a timetable, a list of people involved and the costs of the proposed research.

3.2.1 What is included in the background and rationale section?

In this section, you should discuss the research background to the study – review the relevant research that has taken place in the area. The purpose of this review is not simply to synthesise existing knowledge in the area but to present this information in such a way that it highlights the gap in the research which your proposed research will address. It might help to think of the structure of this review as taking the shape of a funnel. At the beginning, there is a presentation of the broad context in which the area of investigation sits, and as the literature review progresses, the focus of the literature reviewed becomes narrower and more specific to the proposed research topic. In this way, you are guiding the reader from the broad area of interest to the specific issue which needs to be investigated, ultimately finding that the funnel is open at the narrowest point – this is the gap that your proposed research will address. Therefore, a well written literature review will generate a clear rationale for the proposed research in the reader's mind just before you make the rationale and aims of the research explicit. In other words, the content of the research aim and research question/hypothesis should come as no surprise to someone who has read your literature review.

Sometimes you will have developed a research idea in which you are very interested and in which you have invested a considerable amount of time thinking about, for example, the research methods you will employ. However, when you conduct a more comprehensive literature review in the area, you find that someone has recently published a study exactly like the one you are proposing. It might be tempting to ignore this study so that you can stick with your idea. Bear in mind that one of the purposes of this section in your proposal is that you demonstrate a good grasp of relevant literature in the area. Therefore, purposely omitting a research study in order to strengthen the rationale for your study is not ethical and is highly likely to be found out. This also highlights the value of conducting a comprehensive literature review before you invest much time in developing your idea further.

Essentially, the literature review sets the scene for everything else. It should connect very obviously with your rationale, your aims and your research protocol. Therefore, although the literature review is one of the first things you should be doing when developing a research proposal, it should be revisited after you develop each remaining section of the proposal, to ensure the connections are clear.

3.2.2   Should I present research aims or objectives or questions or hypotheses?

This is probably the most important section of your research proposal. As your research idea develops, you will need to convert the idea into a more formal statement of what your proposed research is trying to do. This is necessary to make the specific focus of the research clear and to allow you to think about issues of feasibility (as described in Section 3.1). When the specific focus of the proposed research is not presented in a clear manner, it is difficult, if not impossible, to make a judgement about the most appropriate research methods to employ.

So, how should your focus be presented: as an aim, research question, hypothesis, or something else? Actually, in many cases it will often make sense to employ more than one of these approaches. I think it is always useful to have clear aims and objectives for your proposed research. You may not wish to state these in your research proposal, but you should at least know what the aim of your proposed research is. Therefore, I think the inclusion of a research aim and/or objectives in a research proposal is uncontroversial. There is more uncertainty about the appropriateness of including research questions and/or hypotheses. Examples of research aims are

- to examine the effectiveness of a group cognitive behavioural therapy programme in reducing depressive symptoms;
- to explore the relationship between beliefs about breast cancer and emotional distress.

What is clear is that research hypotheses serve a very specific purpose and, therefore, should probably be reserved for specific situations.

Hypotheses are statements of the expected research findings. Presenting research hypotheses indicates that you are following a hypothetico-deductive approach in your research. In other words, you have hypothesised the outcomes of the research, based on logical deductions guided by theory. Hypotheses are unambiguous about the expected research findings and so should be used only when you feel that justifiable predictions about the research findings can be made. Often, hypotheses will be appropriate in experimental-type designs, such as the evaluation of an intervention. It is highly likely that any intervention which is being used in a 'real-life' setting is based on a considerable amount of previous research and development and that there is evidence that the techniques being employed in the intervention are likely to be effective. In this situation, it would seem reasonable to present a research hypothesis declaring that the intervention will be effective and then conducting the research to test this hypothesis. Examples of research hypotheses follow.

- The relationship between the subjective norm for exercise behaviour and actual exercise behaviour will be mediated by intentions to exercise.
- The group cognitive behavioural therapy intervention will be effective in reducing depressive symptoms between the pre-test to the post-test stages of assessment. (This hypothesis might be presented in addition to the first example of a research aim provided above.)

Alternatively, a research question could be presented when you feel that there is not sufficient information to allow you to make a prediction about the research findings. Research questions are often employed when the proposed research is not developed from existing theory but when it aims to generate new theory, or in other words, when you are proposing to investigate an area in which little research exists or where the research findings are contradictory, or where you believe that the hypothetico-deductive approach to research is narrow and inappropriate to gain an understanding of individual experiences. Research designed to address research questions tends to be of an exploratory nature. It aims to develop an understanding of the data gathered and discern relationships within the data, as opposed to testing a specific hypothesis. Examples of research questions follow.

- To what extent are beliefs about cancer related to psychological distress among women recently diagnosed with breast cancer? (This question might be presented in addition to the second example of a research aim provided above.)

- What are the barriers to seeking preconception care among women with Type 1 Diabetes?

In a sense, presenting a research hypothesis forces you to be precise and focused, and the danger with presenting a research question is that it can be imprecise. This should not be the case. Choosing to present a research question is not a licence to avoid precision or to leave the question broad and then narrow it down when you see what interesting associations can be found in the data. Research questions still require a clear focus, which will direct the research design. In addition, research questions, like research hypotheses, need to be clearly operationalised. That is, clear definitions should be provided (where necessary) of the terms used in the research question/hypothesis.

3.2.3   What does a research protocol contain?

A research protocol is the part of your proposal which states the plan for the conduct of your proposed research. This is where you stipulate how your proposed research will be conducted in order to address the research questions/hypotheses. The research protocol can be thought of as a proposal for the methods section of your final research paper. The research protocol informs the reader about what you are going to do and the methods section in your final report informs the reader about what you did. The research protocol should contain information about the following:

3.2.3.1   The research participants

You should state who the research participants will be. More specifically, you need to provide the inclusion and exclusion criteria that define who will be invited to participate in the research. These inclusion and exclusion criteria should be justifiable, and if the rationale for these criteria is not obvious, it should be made explicit. There should also be a clear statement about where participants will be recruited from, the method of sampling that will be used and how many participants will be recruited (including the expected attrition rate if a longitudinal design is used). These latter issues can be decided only when you have made a decision about your research design. Therefore, further discussion of these issues is presented in Chapters 4, 6 and 7.

The inclusion of a proposed sample size is necessary because including too few participants in your research will, at best, result in unsatisfactory answers to your research question and, at worst, could mean that your research has been pointless. On the other hand, including too many participants in your research means that you are asking people to give up their time and take part in procedures which are unnecessary. Both of these outcomes could be considered unethical. Consequently, ethics committees will often want to see evidence in your research proposal that sample size has been considered. Furthermore, reviewers of your research proposal will want to satisfy themselves that you have considered the consequences of your proposed sample size for your analyses. When proposing quantitative research which aims to use statistical analysis, it is possible to estimate the sample size you are likely to need, based on the statistical power (for studies intending to use inferential statistics) or accuracy (for studies intending to use descriptive statistics) of your study. There are alternative considerations when estimating sample size for qualitative studies or quantitative pilot studies. For qualitative research, the required sample size is driven by the type of methodology employed. In some qualitative research a single case might be appropriate; in other research, a sample size of 20–30 people might be included. It is highly unusual to see sample sizes any larger than this in qualitative research conducted by trainee psychologists. A discussion of the sample size required for qualitative research is provided in Section 6.1.1 and throughout Chapter 7. Further details on calculating sample size for quantitative studies, specific to the type of research design employed, are provided in Section 5.4, and an overview of the principles of sample size calculations based on statistical power is provided in Box 3.1.

Box 3.1 Principles of sample size calculations based on statistical power

A statistical estimation of sample size will be based, to some extent, on your research design (including the number and type of variables to be incorporated) and planned statistical analysis. The estimation will be based also on your desired level of statistical power, alpha and the effect size.

Statistical analysis is based on probability, not certainty. The concepts of statistical power and alpha represent the probability of two different outcomes from your statistical analysis.

Statistical power is the probability that your statistical analysis will reject the null hypothesis when it is false. In other words, statistical

Box 3.1   Continued

power is the likelihood that you will find a statistically significant result which it is correct. Generally, if a null hypothesis is false we want to be quite confident that our analysis will reject it. By convention, therefore, it is preferable to have statistical power of 90 %, although a minimum of 80 % is considered acceptable.

Alpha is the probability that your statistical analysis will reject the null hypothesis when it is true. In other words, alpha is the likelihood that you will find a statistically significant result which is incorrect. Generally, if a null hypothesis is true we want to be confident that our analysis will not reject it. By convention, therefore, the maximum alpha value acceptable is 5 % (this is the 0.05 'cut-off' point that we use to conclude whether a statistical test is significant or not).

Constraints on resources usually mean that when we are proposing research, we are aiming for the minimum sample size necessary. Therefore, it is useful to know that (all other things being equal) the number of people required for your proposed research will decrease as power decreases and alpha increases. So when calculating sample size, researchers will often base the calculation on an alpha of 0.05 (or 5 %) and statistical power of 0.8 (or 80 %). To calculate sample size for a specified research design and particular statistical analysis the only thing left to decide on is the effect size.

The concept of an effect size, along with some examples, is explained in Section 2.4. Basically, an effect size is an indication of the size of the effect expected in your research (for example, the magnitude of the correlation between two variables or the size of the differences between groups or the value of the R^2 statistic in a regression model that you will expect to find in your proposed research). The smaller the effect size expected, the larger the sample size that will be required (all else being held constant). The difficulty here is that it is relatively easy to calculate an effect size when you have data, but you are being asked to estimate the likely effect size at the proposal stage of the research. Therefore, you have several options.

- Use data from a pilot study to calculate an effect size.
- Use data reported in similar previously published studies to calculate effect size.

Box 3.1   Continued

- Estimate an effect size based on the minimum effect size which is considered to be important, that is, the minimum effect that represents something clinically important. This is sometimes referred to as the minimum clinically important difference or as the threshold for clinical significance. The idea here is that you are ensuring that you have a sufficient sample size to detect any clinically relevant effects but not any effects smaller than this, on the basis that effects smaller than this are not important in a clinical setting. For example, if you are proposing to evaluate an intervention which aims to reduce hospital readmissions for a particular patient group, then clinicians working in the area will be a vital source of information in helping you to work out the minimum reduction in number of hospital admissions that would be considered to be indicative of a meaningful change in the patient group. Alternatively, your outcome measure might be scores on a questionnaire. In this case, you want to know the minimum change on the questionnaire score that would be considered meaningful. Again, clinicians with experience in using this questionnaire might be able to help with this decision. Bearing in mind that scores can change as a result of measurement error alone, it is worth factoring in the standard error of measurement of your questionnaire when considering the amount of change that is clinically important (see Section 4.2).
- If you cannot estimate a specific effect size, then you should estimate whether you expect the effect to be small, medium or large (and develop an argument that justifies your decision). You can then convert this into an effect size value using standard guidelines, depending on the analysis you intend to use. For example, when using correlation coefficients, the guidelines are that small, medium and large effect sizes are represented by correlation coefficients of 0.1, 0.3 and 0.5 respectively. Further guidelines are presented under the discussions of sample size in Section 5.4.

Bear in mind that a statistician can help with the calculation of sample size but might not be familiar with the relevant research in your area. Therefore, it is up to you (and your supervisor) to make decisions about the likely effect size to be expected.

3.2.3.2 The research materials/instruments

The materials to be used in the research will also vary greatly, depending on the type of research proposed. The materials could be a piece of equipment, such as a computer package or equipment to gather psychophysiological data; they could be questionnaires or psychological tests; or they could be interview schedules/guides. An appropriate description for each type of material is required as part of the research protocol. The description of technical equipment should include the manufacturer and model, but in addition to that the rationale for inclusion of this equipment and the amount of additional information provided will depend on the type of equipment you propose to use and the amount of controversy in the area about different models. It will be very important in this situation to work with a supervisor who is experienced in using the proposed equipment and is aware of any issues that exist with choosing different models. When proposing to use questionnaires, tests or interview schedules in your research, more generic guidance can be provided; this is discussed in Section 4.2.

3.2.3.3 The research procedure

Essentially, this is a description of the method by which participants will be recruited to the study and what will happen to them once they agree to participate. A briefer and non-technical version of the research procedure should be provided to potential participants before they agree to participate in the research, to ensure that they know what they are agreeing to do (see Section 3.3).

The description of the method of recruitment should be a detailed, sequential description of how and by whom potential participants will be identified, how and by whom the inclusion/exclusion criteria will be applied, how and where participants will be approached and informed about the study, who will approach them and in what format the information about the study will be provided. There should be an indication of the time lag between someone being given information about the study and being asked for their decision about whether they will agree to participate. The method by which participants provide consent to participate in the study, who obtains this consent and how this consent is recorded should be clarified in the protocol. Issues surrounding this procedure are discussed in Section 3.3.

The design of the research and procedures for data collection should be described in this section of the proposal. The description of the research design needs to be a description rather than a label. For example, stating that the research will follow an experimental design is of limited value and not very helpful unless it is followed by a more detailed description of what this specific experiment will look like (Chapters 4, 6 and 7 discuss the important characteristics of research design which should be considered at this stage and during the conduct of the research). Nevertheless, standard ethics application forms often ask you to label your research design, and Box 3.2 provides a definition of research designs currently referred to on the Integrated Research Application System (IRAS) form (see Section 3.3 for a discussion of the IRAS form). Box 3.2 does not include mixed methods designs, even though this type of research design has found increasing popularity in health research in recent years. Mixed methods designs can refer to a programme of research that includes both qualitative and quantitative studies or a single study that aims to gather both qualitative and quantitative data (sometimes called mixed model research).

Box 3.2 Research designs in the IRAS form

The terminologies used in the IRAS form are not intended to be mutually exclusive, so you might find that your proposed study meets more than one of the following definitions. For example, the research question 'to what extent are beliefs about cancer related to psychological distress among women recently diagnosed with breast cancer?' might lead to a research study that can be classified as a 'cohort study' and a 'questionnaire, interview or observation study'.

Case series/case note review

A (usually) detailed analysis of information held in case notes of a homogeneous group of individuals. Often the term 'case study' is used when this analysis is conducted to a deeper level with a single case.

Case control

Case-control studies are used to compare two groups of participants –'cases' and 'controls'. The cases are individuals who, for example, have been exposed to some intervention, have been diagnosed with some condition, or have engaged in a particular action/ behaviour. The key defining feature here is that the cases are

Box 3.2   Continued

identified retrospectively. In other words, participants are defined
by whether they have the outcome of interest, and then we examine
potential predictors of this outcome. If we recruit participants before
the outcome is known with the aim of observing whether the outcome
develops, this is a cohort study (see below). Conclusions drawn from
case control studies are strengthened if the controls are matched to
the cases. For example, by looking at the histories of people with lung
cancer (cases) and a matched group of people without lung cancer
(controls), we might see that before their diagnosis of lung cancer
there was a higher rate of smoking among the cases, leading to the
conclusion that smoking is a risk factor for lung cancer.

Cohort observation

Often referred to as a longitudinal survey design by psychologists, this
is a longitudinal study in which a group (or cohort) of people defined
by some characteristic (such as year of birth (birth cohort), diagnosis)
are assessed on the measures of interest over time. A control group
is often included. Cohort studies (with or without controls) can be
current or historical. For example, a current cohort study might recruit
a large number of people, some of whom will be smokers, and follow
them over time, assessing their health and the incidence of lung
cancer; a historical cohort study might identify smokers and non-
smokers from records and then follow their recorded history to assess
their health and the incidence of lung cancer (all of which will have
already happened). Historical cohort studies are often confused with
case-control studies. The difference is that in a historical cohort study,
people are identified on the basis of their recorded predictor variables
and then information is sought about outcomes whereas in a case-
control study, people are identified on the basis of their outcomes
and then information is sought about their predictor variables.

Controlled trial without randomisation

Participants are allocated to one of two (or more) groups in a non-
random manner. At least one group experiences an intervention, and
at least one group is a control or comparison group (for example,
people on a waiting list for treatment are used as a control group
and compared to those receiving treatment). Outcomes are assessed

Box 3.2 Continued

at least before and after the intervention phase. Psychologists might refer to this as a type of quasi-experimental design.

Cross-sectional study

A research design where measures are obtained from participants at one point in time (as compared to a longitudinal study where measures are obtained from the same participants at more than one point in time).

Database analysis

An analysis of data which have already been collected and which have been collated and stored – often referred to as secondary data analysis.

Epidemiology

A population-based study which aims to establish risk factors for disease by examining associations between hypothesised causes of the disease and disease incidence/prevalence.

Feasibility/pilot study

A study designed to assess aspects of the research method (e.g. data collection procedures) and the type of data obtained in order to determine whether a full scale study is warranted or to obtain essential information before a full scale study can be conducted.

Laboratory study

A study conducted in a laboratory setting which is usually biomedical.

Meta-analysis

A systematic review (see Chapter 2).

Qualitative research

Any research which primarily aims to obtain qualitative data (see Chapters 6 and 7).

Questionnaire, interview or observation study

Any research which uses questionnaires, interviews or observational methods to collect data.

Box 3.2   Continued

Randomised controlled trial

Participants are randomly allocated to one of two (or more) groups. At least one group experiences an intervention, and at least one group is a control or comparison group. Outcomes are assessed at least before and after the intervention phase. Psychologists might refer to this as a type of experimental design.

The procedures for data collection should outline when and where data will be collected, any time delays between data collection points (if appropriate), who will collect the data, and what participants will be asked to do to provide this data (including some estimate of the burden this will impose on participants at least in terms of their time).

3.2.4   How detailed should the data analysis plan be?

In some cases, your data analysis plan can be only an outline of your approach to the data analysis, but you need to have some idea of the type of analysis that you are likely to undertake. There are two reasons for this. Firstly, it indicates that you believe that your research design and materials will provide data in a format necessary to allow you to address the research aim. Secondly, when you are conducting quantitative research, you need to have a sense of the likely statistical procedures that will be employed before you can estimate the sample size required for your research.

Of course, once your data has been collected, it may require you to revise your data analysis plans. For example, with quantitative data, the distribution of your data may not lend itself to analysis by the parametric tests you have proposed, at least not without some manipulation of the data, so there are decisions here which will need to be finalised in light of the data obtained. Nevertheless, your approach to the analysis and the aim of the analysis will remain the same even though the specific techniques employed might change, and, therefore, you should delineate your approach to the data analysis in your proposal.

Data analysis plans tend to operate on a very clear quantitative bias. Basically, where traditional statistical techniques are to be employed (for example, analysis of variance, regression), it generally appears to be acceptable to state these without any further discussion or justification. However, when qualitative data is to be analysed, a justification of the approach chosen and the details of the data analysis procedure appears to be the norm. My experience of this bias is that it actually benefits trainees who are proposing qualitative research. When a good qualitative research proposal is presented, the critique of the planned data analysis results in a data analysis strategy which is more obviously 'owned' by the trainee proposing the research. This is something which the trainee has considered carefully, including weighing up other approaches to the analysis of their data and which the trainee can often verbalise clearly. It is refreshing to encounter a trainee who can discuss the epistemology driving their data analysis approach, and this often results in fewer problems when it comes to implementing the data analysis strategy. Unfortunately, data analysis plans for quantitative research are often based on some algorithm which asks about your research design and research question and then tells you what statistical analysis is most appropriate. Consequently, this is often not something which the trainee spends time considering, until their data is collected, and it is at that stage that problems arise. Sometimes these problems are insurmountable as they would have required some modification to the data collection procedure.

Before writing a data analysis plan, I suggest that you familiarise yourself with some of the general data analysis procedures for quantitative and qualitative data (see Chapters 5 and 6 respectively).

3.2.5 Do I need to include anything else in the proposal?

Sections 3.2.1–3.2.4 expanded on the main elements of a research proposal. As mentioned earlier, the proposal should probably also contain the following, perhaps as an appendix to the main proposal:

- *Dissemination plans.* Indicate where the final report will be disseminated. For example, name a peer-reviewed journal if appropriate. There may also be a particular conference at which you will wish to present the information.
- *A timetable.* This should indicate the main tasks that will be conducted between submission of the proposal and the completion of the research, at least on a monthly basis. It should make provision for the time required to negotiate the research governance and ethics procedures and for your supervisor(s) to read and provide feedback on a draft of your final report, as well as allowing you time to integrate this feedback, before the date of submission.
- *The people who are involved in the research and their agreed roles in the research.* This is particularly important when you are relying on someone else to help you access participants or collect data. Their

co-operation is crucial to the successful completion of the research, so anyone scrutinising your proposal will want to know that this co-operation has been secured (preferably in a formal way).

- *Costs.* You should provide some estimate of the likely costs of the research. Costs might include things such as paper and photocopying costs, travel expenses for you and/or your participants, refreshments for participants, the costs of obtaining questionnaires, tests or other equipment, postage costs, room hire costs and so on.
- *References.* Include a reference list for any citations in your proposal.
- *Study materials.* This will include, for example, questionnaires, information sheets and consent forms.

At this point, trainees will often ask how long the proposal should be. The answer will sometimes be specified by your particular training programme, but in the absence of any specific information, perhaps the guidance provided by the Economic Social Research Council (ESRC) and the Medical Research Council (MRC) could be helpful. The ESRC indicates that six A4 sides (no smaller than font size point 12) should be sufficient for the entire research proposal (not including the elements in the bullet points above); the MRC suggests eight A4 sides should be sufficient. Obviously these are general guidelines, and you need to consider the important issues that need to be highlighted in your proposal, and take whatever space is needed to present these issues in a concise manner.

The guidance presented in this section is general advice. There are many issues to be considered in detail before a research proposal can be completed, and to make appropriate decisions you need to ensure that you are appropriately informed. The remainder of this book aims to provide a more detailed discussion of the key issues to be considered when planning and conducting different types of qualitative and quantitative research.

3.3 Research governance and ethics

The purpose of this section is not to discuss the ethical principles underpinning the good conduct of research, which I am sure you are familiar with, but to discuss the questions that trainees often ask about the process of obtaining ethics approval for a research proposal which is to be conducted in the field of health and/or social care.

The process of obtaining ethics approval for health/social care research can appear complex the first time you encounter it, as it is strewn with legislation, scrutiny committees and other obstacles that need to be negotiated. Often, it feels like you are being asked questions that are irrelevant to your research, that some of the people asking these questions do not really understand your answers and that there is a level of pedanticism present which can only serve to discourage people from engaging in applied research. However, in the spirit of a good psychologist, the situation will become clearer and more understandable if you spend a little time trying to understand why the process exists in its current form and, consequently, why individuals on scrutiny committees appear obsessed with certain types of questions and level of details.

Obtaining research ethics approval for health/social care research was not always as burdensome for the researcher. Until the 21st century, it was largely assumed that researchers working in the health/social care field (usually health professionals) could be trusted to conduct research in an ethical manner. Indeed, even after the establishment of the first research ethics committees in the UK (in the later half of the 20th century), researchers were not legally obliged to obtain approval from these committees, and, therefore, the process was still mostly based on trust. Unfortunately, some high profile cases towards the end of the 20th century highlighted that some (medical) researchers were, at best, guilty of errors of judgement when it came to making decisions about ethical practice. Therefore, the UK government introduced legislation to ensure that the ethics of proposed health/social care research were considered by a committee of independent people before the research was allowed to proceed. At the time of writing, the work of the ethics committees for research conducted in the NHS is now overseen by the National Research Ethics Service (NRES), which has replaced the previously established Central Office for Research Ethics Committees (COREC).

The legislation introduced by the UK government to govern approval of health research is largely focused on trials of medicinal products or other medical interventions. This type of research is likely to cause harm to participants if it is not conducted in an ethical and safe manner, and it is also often undertaken by pharmaceutical companies, who have a vested interest in the results of the research. Therefore, it seems appropriate that government would be primarily concerned with protecting the public participating in this type of research. The downside of this is that many of the standard questions that were asked on the NRES ethics application form assumed that you were conducting research which aimed to evaluate a drug, using a design such as a randomised controlled trial. This situation has improved considerably more recently, although you will find a small number of questions on the NRES ethics application form that reflect this historical position. This can be a potential source of problems if you are proposing a research study which does not conform to the template that the Research Ethics Committee (REC) members have in mind.

However, on the positive side, the system is changing and has changed. As RECs become aware of different research designs, as more psychologists become part of RECs, as psychologists learn the language of the biomedical researcher and as RECs begin to realise that psychological research is not more likely to result in harm to participants than other types of research, then we have begun to be able to communicate more effectively with each other. The research ethics application form is also constantly changing and is now much more user friendly to psychological research. The upshot of this is that, in my experience, it is now considerably easier to progress a psychological research proposal through the NHS ethics process than it was five years ago.

Of course, the current system of ethics approval is still largely based on trust (even though penalties can be imposed for serious breaches). We trust that researchers will bring their research proposals forward for scrutiny before their research begins, and we trust that researchers will not change their research protocol once it has been given ethics approval. Therefore, obtaining ethics approval will not and could not replace the need for self-monitoring and ensuring that your practice adheres to the appropriate ethical standards.

It is worth mentioning at this point that the structure and nomenclature of NRES, the requirements for obtaining ethics approval and the forms used for this purpose have been undergoing continual change over recent years. Much of this change is positive (as mentioned earlier), but this means that you need to ensure that you are following the latest procedures and guidelines and completing the most recent version of the ethics application form when applying for ethics approval through NRES. Because of the dynamic nature of the arrangements for obtaining ethics approval, I have not included any examples of completed ethics approval forms – they would likely be outdated by the time you read this book! Instead, I have tried to provide some guidelines which should be more resistant to change over time.

3.3.1 *What do i need to do to get NRES ethics approval?*

If you need to get NRES ethics approval, then it is likely that you will also need approval for your research from your local NHS Research & Development (R&D) office. If you are conducting your research as part of a training programme within a university setting, then you may also need research approval from the university, or the university may have an arrangement for providing joint approval with the local NHS R&D office. Apart from securing these approvals from the different bodies, you will also need a sponsor for your research. The research sponsor takes responsibility for initiating, financing and managing a study. Normally, the sponsor will be the employer of the chief investigator for the study, such as a university or local NHS Trust.

Obviously, there are a number of bodies involved in scrutinising and approving your proposal before your research can begin, and it is this inter-play which can often cause confusion for trainees. To add to the confusion, slightly different processes may operate in Northern Ireland, Scotland, England and Wales, and slightly different processes may operate in different universities, so you need to make yourself aware of any local peculiarities. Consulting your supervisor and clarifying the process with the local NHS Trust Research Officer and your university's Research Governance Officer (if appropriate) is a very good idea at an early stage in the process. You might need to do a little bit of research to find out who the local NHS Trust Research Officer is, which REC is the most appropriate for your research and your geographical area, and who the local REC contact is. The general process should look something like that outlined in Box 3.3.

There are some points to bear in mind when reading the process in Box 3.3:

- Your university might also require you to make a formal ethics application to a university committee. In some cases, the university might only require you to notify them of a successful REC review; in other situations, the university ethics committee might fulfil the peer review role mentioned in the first point in Box 3.3. Ensure that you know what local procedures are required.
- The NHS Trust might also be the sponsor of the research. If this is the case, then this should be discussed with the NHS Trust Research Officer before making a formal application for approval of the research.
- Applications to the NHS Trust and the REC are made using the Integrated Research Application System (IRAS) form (www.myresearchproject.org.uk).
- When applying to the NHS Trust, you should send the R&D version of the IRAS form, along with a site specific information (SSI) form, your research proposal, the fully completed submission checklist (available on the IRAS site) and anything else required by the NHS Trust Research Officer (such as local Trust forms which ask about the details of the financing of the proposed research). Ensure that any relevant materials requested on the checklist are included in your application.
- When applying to the REC, you should send the REC version of the IRAS form, your research proposal and the fully completed sub-mission checklist (available on the IRAS website). Ensure that any

relevant materials requested on the checklist are included in your application.
- At the time of writing, applications to the REC and applications to the NHS Trust can be made simultaneously.

Box 3.3   Research governance and ethics approval process

- Obtain satisfactory peer reviews of your research proposal (this may require you to make revisions to your proposal based on feedback before you obtain final satisfactory peer review). Your supervisor or training programme may organise peer review for you. Applications for research approval cannot be considered without first obtaining satisfactory peer review.
- Make initial contact with the local NHS Trust Research Officer (and University Research Governance Officer if appropriate) to alert them to the project and enquire about any specific requirements, e.g. honorary contract/research passport and good clinical practice awareness training.
- Obtain a sponsorship agreement from the research sponsor. This must be obtained before you progress any further in the process. The sponsor may require you to complete specific forms or submit specific information before agreeing to sponsor the research. Therefore, you need to allow time to complete this process before you can make any further applications to the NHS Trust or REC (as they both require written agreement from the sponsor).
- Apply to the local NHS Trust Research Office for research approval.
- Apply to the local NHS REC for ethics approval.
- If necessary, send required revisions to the local NHS REC (copy to NHS Trust and sponsor), and await notice of favourable ethics opinion.
- Once a favourable ethics opinion has been obtained, clarify with Trust and sponsor that final approval has been obtained.
- If necessary, complete an annual progress report using NRES form (copy to NHS Trust and sponsor)
- Send notice of any substantial amendments to local NHS REC (copy to NHS Trust and sponsor)
- Complete 'End of Study' declaration using NRES form (copy to NHS Trust and sponsor)

3.3.2 Do I need to obtain NRES ethics approval?

It depends on the nature of your proposed research. The approval process outlined in the previous section is specific to NHS-based research in the UK or research conducted in England or Wales which involves adults lacking capacity to consent for themselves. Therefore, if your proposed research does not fall under this definition, there is no need for you to follow this process (although you should check that this situation has not changed since the time of writing this book). Additionally, if you are not conducting research, as defined by NRES, then there is no need to follow this process. However, the type of work conducted for a major research project in the training of clinical and health psychologists usually falls within this definition of research. The type of work which falls outside this definition is discussed in Chapter 8.

So, how do you know if your research is NHS based? By NHS-based research, I mean research which recruits participants via an NHS service or which recruits NHS staff as participants or which takes place on NHS property. By using the term NHS, I am including the health services provided in England, Scotland and Wales and the Health and Social Care services in Northern Ireland. However, some applied research falls outside this definition. For example, you may wish to recruit your participants from a patient support group which is an independent charity. In this case, the process outlined in Box 3.3 does not apply.

However, all research should have a sponsor, be subject to research governance arrangements and ethics approval. Therefore, avoiding the NHS system does not necessarily reduce the burden on the researcher at this stage. For example, if you are recruiting participants through a patient support group you might need to apply to a research governance and ethics committee within the charity and an ethics committee within your institution. Although there is often less bureaucracy associated with ethics-approval processes outside the NHS, sometimes the processes are less efficient and information about the process and what is required from you might be difficult to find.

3.3.3 Why would my research proposal be given an unfavourable ethics opinion?

It might be surprising to realise that an ethics application can be unsuccessful (given an unfavourable opinion), after it has been given satisfactory peer review, and perhaps scrutinised by a sponsor and a NHS Trust Research Committee. This is because different bodies scrutinise the proposal with a different aim in mind. You might have constructed a research proposal which is scientifically sound and which does not pose any risks for the Trust or the sponsor (in their opinion) but which raises some ethical dilemmas for the REC. Of course, it is hard to predict what issues will cause concern for the members of the REC, as this will depend on who on the REC reads your proposal. Nevertheless, there are some recurrent themes which are worth paying attention to, so that your chances of receiving an unfavourable opinion are minimised.

Clearly, it is important to ensure that the research proposed follows sound ethical principles, such as that detailed in the BPS Code of Ethics and Conduct (http://www.bps.org.uk/sites/default/files/documents/code_of_ethics_and_conduct.pdf). However, there are more specific issues to applied research in the health/social care field that are often the cause of ethics applications being unsuccessful. These issues tend to focus on the areas of recruitment of participants, the potential for distress resulting from participation in the research, and the storage of data. So, I suggest that when completing an NRES ethics application, you pay particular attention to the following:

- *The method of identifying potential participants.* In your research proposal, you will have stated inclusion and exclusion criteria for potential participants in the study. You also then need to indicate how people will be assessed against these criteria and identified as potential participants for your research and who will undertake this task. As a straightforward example, imagine that for your proposed research you need participants who are adults and have been diagnosed with ischemic heart disease within the past 12 months. There is no way of identifying people who received the required diagnosis within the past 12 months unless you have access to their medical history. If you are working with ischemic heart disease patients as part of their care team, then you will have access to this information. However, more often than not, trainees are not in this situation. Consequently, someone else who is part of the care team and has access to medical information needs to be involved in the identification of participants.
- *The method of recruitment of participants.* Once someone appropriate has identified potential participants, how will these people be approached and asked to participate in the research and who will do this? It is often not appropriate for a list of potential participants to be provided to you, as this provides you with specific medical information about people which is meant to be confidential. In general, this leaves two options: (1) potential participants are asked for their consent for their contact details to be passed to you

to allow you to invite them to participate in the research or (2) the person who identifies the potential participants invites them to participate in the research. There are dilemmas to be considered in both options. In brief, following option (1) creates a two-step consent process which is time consuming and leads to a higher risk of drop-outs; following option (2) means that the person involved in the potential participants' care is issuing the invitation to take part in the research and this might be construed as coercion. Therefore, strategies need to be put in place to alleviate these concerns. For example, it could be the case that you are recruiting participants from an outpatients' clinic. In this case, the potential participants are issued an invitation by their health care professional and then told that if they might like to participate, they should speak with you (in a different room). In this way, you have no contact with the participant until they have decided to at least find out more about the research and the health professional is not asking for consent. Furthermore, the person's decision to participate in the research is then hidden from the clinician, which means that the person's decision and their participation in the research is clearly separated from the care they are receiving.

- *The method of invitation.* We have just discussed who should issue the invitation to participate in the research. In addition, the specific content of the invitation also needs to be considered. There is an expectation that the invitation to participate in research will be issued in a written form, known as a participant information sheet (PIS). A poster or advertisement might be used to initially invite participants, but when people respond to this they will then need to be issued with a PIS. RECs will be concerned with the exact form of words used in the PIS and any poster or advertisement. Potential participants should be given time to fully consider the information provided on the PIS and to ask any further questions about the research before being asked for their consent to participate. This consent is usually obtained in written form and, again, RECs will want to scrutinise the consent form that you propose to use. Guidance on the structure and completion of a PIS and consent form is provided by NRES and can be found at http://www.nres.npsa.nhs.uk/applications/guidance/, along with other useful information. Remember that this guidance is generic, with a bias towards evaluations of medical interventions, so you will need to make some adaptations to make this information relevant to your proposed research.

- *Procedures for dealing with distress.* In my experience, many of the members of RECs are uncomfortable with the idea of asking participants questions about psychological distress or traumatic events. There sometimes appears to be an assumption that if you ask people about their level of distress, this will cause them to become distressed and then this will need to be dealt with. Not surprisingly, then, RECs are often concerned that psychological research has a strong potential to leave participants feeling distressed. Of course, the assumption is not accurate, but there is still an onus on you to demonstrate that either your research will not cause the participant to become distressed or that there are procedures in place to deal with participant distress if this occurs. In my experience, when dealing with research about trauma or psychological distress, it is probably best to do both these things. So you need to cite previous similar research that has been conducted without any adverse events for participants and/or cite research demonstrating the value of participation in this type of research (for example, Ruzek & Zatzick, 2000; Griffin, Resick, Waldrop & Mechanic, 2003; Form, Kelly & Morgan, 2007). Additionally, you need to outline the pathway that will be used in the unlikely event that participants are distressed by participation in the research. This will involve providing contact details of an appropriate person that participants can contact should they become distressed and the name of a person (such as an appropriately trained psychologist) to whom the participants could then be referred. I think it is also important to make a distinction between distress that is caused by participation in the research and distress which is already present and which might be the topic of the research. As researchers we must ensure that we minimise the risk of causing distress to any participants and that we have procedures in place to deal with the unlikely situation where this occurs. However, we should not be expected to provide participants who are already experiencing distress with a shortcut to therapy because they have participated in our research (although you should have a protocol for managing this distress during the research process to ensure it is not exacerbated and to deal with any causes for concern such as an indication that the participant intends to harm themselves or someone else).

- *Dealing with personal data.* RECs also tend to pay particular attention to the treatment of any data obtained from participants (both personal data and research data). They will want to be reassured that data and any signed consent forms are stored securely and confidentially and that the principles of data protection are being adhered to. They will want to know how long personal data will be stored, who will be responsible for it and how it will be destroyed.

You should make this clear in your REC application and highlight any encryption procedures that will be used if data are to be transported electronically. RECs will want to know whether the data you obtain are anonymous or whether they will be anonymised. If they are to be anonymised you will need to clarify the procedures for this. It is worth seeking advice from your institution, which might have a policy on the storage of data.

Summary – developing an applied research proposal

Identify a research idea of interest

Review the relevant background literature

Establish a clear rationale for your research idea

Make an initial assessment of the feasibility of this idea

Refine and specify the research question

Write a research proposal detailing the research design and methods, methods of recruitment of participants and any research materials/instruments to be used

Obtain satisfactory peer reviews of your proposals

Obtain a sponsorship agreement from the research sponsor

Obtain approval from the NHS Trust and NHS Research Ethics Committee (and University if appropriate)

4

Designing Quantitative Research

• •

As indicated in Chapter 3, the design and methods of your research project need to be considered at the proposal stage of the research process. In psychology, you will often find that research designs are grouped into experimental (and quasi-experimental) designs, survey designs and qualitative designs. While this broad categorisation of research designs can be useful, it does not indicate the subtle (and not so subtle) differences that exist between different research designs included under any one of these headings.

This chapter is not a discussion of the details of all research designs (there are other research methods books which perform this task admirably and I am assuming a certain level of familiarity with these designs, given that you will all have completed an undergraduate psychology programme). Rather the chapter aims to highlight some of the issues that you might need to think about when conducting health-related psychological research, which follows an experimental, quasi-experimental or survey design and which aims to collect quantitative data (Chapter 6 addresses the designs of qualitative research).

By an experimental or quasi-experimental research design, I am intending to mean research which is designed to evaluate the effectiveness of an intervention. In both cases, it is usual to find at least an intervention group and a control or comparison group, and outcomes are assessed at least prior to the administration of the intervention (pre-test or baseline) and after completion of the intervention (post-test) in both groups. A true experimental design is where the researcher has control over which participants are allocated to which of the study groups and where the researcher is able to manipulate the independent variable (intervention). Quasi-experimental designs are experimental designs where the researcher does not have control over participant allocation and/or the intervention.

Within experimental and quasi-experimental designs, a control group is a group which does not receive any intervention/treatment (sometimes referred to as level zero of the independent variable) whereas a comparison group is a group which receives some level of treatment different from that received by the intervention group. An example of a research hypothesis for an experimental type study was presented in Chapter 3: 'The group cognitive behavioural therapy intervention will be effective in reducing depressive symptoms between the pre-test to the post-test stages of assessment'. We might assess the effectiveness of the intervention by comparing the results from the intervention group to a control group that receives no intervention or to a comparison group that receives a different type of intervention, such as bibliotherapy. The choice of a control or comparison group will be directed by your research question (although the decision is often imposed by the constraints on your research project), and the differences between the two are important as they will affect your conclusions.

By a survey design, I am intending to mean research which is designed to examine relationships or associations between variables. This type of research does not involve interventions with participants and does not aim to manipulate variables. Rather its aim is to measure variables of interest as they occur and to examine the extent to which variables co-vary. An example of a research question for a survey design was presented in Chapter 3: 'To what extent are beliefs about cancer related to psychological distress among women recently diagnosed with breast cancer?' When surveys are conducted longitudinally, they can also indicate how a variable measured at one point in time predicts the occurrence of a different variable measured at a later point in time. This type of research is useful in helping us explain variables of interest and thereby build models which suggest the paths of action between variables.

The remainder of this chapter aims to provide a guide to how the quality of the design of experimental, quasi-experimental or survey type research can be maximised.

4.1 Study validity/quality

The quality of a study is a term often used to refer to an overall assessment of how well the study was designed, conducted and reported. You will, of course, want to aim for a high quality study, and this is what any assessors of your research will be expecting. The criteria on which the quality of a study design and methods are assessed are the extent to which the study maximises internal and/or external validity.

4.1.1 How can I maximise internal validity in my study design?

A study is high in internal validity when the design allows you to draw strong cause-and-effect conclusions. Therefore, high internal validity is desired in particular when conducting research which aims to evaluate interventions, that is, experimental or quasi-experimental research designs. Basically, you will achieve high internal validity if you can control all the factors which could affect the outcomes of the research. In theory, if you can hold all other relevant factors constant and manipulate the variable of interest (the intervention or independent variable) then any changes in the outcome measure (the dependent variable) must be due to this manipulation. In this situation, we could happily conclude that the intervention (or independent variable) causes the outcomes detected.

Not surprisingly, things are not that simple in applied psychological research. There are many factors which could affect the outcomes of your research and over which you will have no direct control. So it is important that you try to identify as many of these factors (extraneous or confounding variables) as possible and build procedures into your research design in order to address these extraneous or confounding variables. The specific extraneous or confounding variables which might be relevant for you will depend on the nature of your proposed research project. The following categories should be useful in helping you to think about these potential threats to internal validity (based on Cook & Campbell, 1979).

4.1.1.1 Attrition

This can threaten internal validity if the people who drop out of your study are different, on relevant variables, from the people who remain in the study. For example, it might be the case that the intervention is ineffective for some people, and, as a result of experiencing no benefit, these people drop out of the research study. Consequently, the effect of the intervention is exaggerated as the people who remain in the study and contribute data for analysis are those most likely to experience a benefit. This effect can be further complicated by differential attrition rates between groups.

It is always useful to demonstrate that attrition is unlikely to have affected the findings of your study by conducting analysis which shows that there were no important differences between those who completed the study and those who did not (this is discussed further in Chapter 9). However, the problem with waiting until the analysis stage is that if you find that there was a difference between 'completers' and 'non-completers', it is too late to do anything about it. Therefore, you need to consider this potential problem at the design stage. Some of the issues you need to consider are: participant burden – how can you minimise this to encourage people to remain in the study; time delay between data collection periods – what is the optimal time to allow change to manifest in participants but without waiting too long so that some participants move away, die or lose interest in the study; reminders – is it possible to remind people to attend to the data collection; enhancing motivation – is it possible to remind participants about the importance of the study and the value of their individual contribution without appearing coercive?

4.1.1.2 Diffusion of the intervention

This refers to a situation where the intervention affects participants in the study who were not meant to receive the intervention (a control or comparison group). Obviously, this can threaten internal validity as it will dilute the effect of the intervention. For example, I supervised a trainee psychologist who was conducting research to examine the effect of a behavioural counselling intervention on the dietary behaviour of people who were attending a cardiac rehabilitation programme. The intervention was to be delivered in a one-to-one setting over a number of weeks and the obvious design for the research was a randomised controlled trial (an experimental design). However, we quickly realised that randomly allocating participants to an intervention group or control group would pose a potential problem of diffusion of the intervention. In other words, there was a potential for the people who were receiving the intervention to return to the cardiac rehabilitation group and talk to others about the content of the intervention, thereby 'contaminating' the participants in the control group. Therefore, we decided to conduct a cluster-randomised control trial, where groups of participants were randomly allocated to the intervention or the control group, meaning that either everyone in a group received the one-to-one intervention or everyone in the group did not receive the intervention. This is a useful design solution, but requires a larger sample size than a simple randomised controlled trial (and a statistician to help you work out the sample size).

4.1.1.3 Events in the environment

This refers to events that occur during the course of the research which could potentially affect the outcomes. Environmental events could be major events occurring at the societal level, or more minor events such as a fire alarm during the data collection procedure. In these cases, we are referring to events that affect everyone in the study and which are usually outside your control. Consequently, there is little that can be done to prevent these events and the solution is often to re-run the study to determine the extent to which these events have impacted your findings, or (where time does not permit) highlight the potential effect of the external event in your discussion of the findings. Re-running a data collection session requires extra time and is one of the reasons you should always build a time contingency into your timetable.

4.1.1.4 Instrument changes

Evaluation of interventions necessitates measuring outcomes at more than one point in time and comparing the measurements obtained at the different time points to determine whether any change is evident. It should be obvious that if there are any changes to the instrument used to collect data at the different points in time, then the data from each time point may not be directly comparable. At first glance, this does not appear to be a difficult threat to avoid. However, subtle changes in how the instrument is presented to participants (for example, the words of introduction used by the researcher when asking participants to complete a questionnaire) can influence the findings. Additionally, when outcomes are assessed through observation, then differences between observers or within an observer can affect the outcomes of the study. The solution to this is to include a clear, standardised protocol for data collection procedures in your research proposal. If necessary, the protocol could be piloted to identify potential sources of problem.

This problem is attenuated when instrument changes apply to one group in the study but not to another. For example, a researcher may provide subtle and unintentional cues to participants which encourage them to respond in a particular manner. In cases where a researcher has invested a great deal of time in developing an intervention and where they have a strong desire to show it to be effective, this may be transmitted to participants. Therefore, internal validity is enhanced by blinding the researcher to the status of the participants, where possible. In other words, the researcher does not know whether the participant has received the intervention or not.

A further potential threat to internal validity which should be included under this heading is the concept of response shift. Response shift arises when a participant is asked to complete a data collection instrument at one point in time and then complete the instrument again at a later point in time after having received some intervention. As a result of this intervention, the participant's perception and evaluation of their environment may change and, consequently, the frame of reference they use when completing the data collection instrument is different from the frame of reference they used when they had first completed the data collection instrument. This means that the results from the data collection points are not comparable because the participant has undergone a change which affects how they think about formulating their responses. For an example of how response shift influences evaluations, see Dempster, Carney and McClements (2010).

4.1.1.5   Maturation

Maturation refers to processes that take place within the individual participants. For example, in a longitudinal assessment of changes in behaviour among children, you would aim to be able to separate natural developmental changes in the children from the changes caused by the intervention. This can often be achieved by the inclusion of a matched control group.

4.1.1.6   Participant reactivity

As students of psychology, you will be familiar with the Hawthorne effect – the idea that participants will react in a particular manner because they are being studied, not because of any intervention. Consequently, there is a need to make your data collection procedures as unobtrusive as possible. There is also a need to consider the extent to which you make your hypotheses clear to participants. It is essential that participants provide informed consent before participating in the study, but sometimes it is possible to indicate to participants what will happen to them without explicitly stating the study hypothesis. Indeed, sometimes providing a study hypothesis will not serve to inform participants but to confuse them, thereby defeating the purpose of providing an information sheet for the study.

Previously, I highlighted the importance of 'blinding' the researcher to the status of the participant. To help avoid participant reactivity, you might be able to create a situation where the participant is unaware of the level of the independent variable they have received. In cases where both the participant and the researcher are 'blinded', we refer to this as a double-blind procedure.

4.1.1.7 Selection bias

Internal validity of a study is high when the only difference between the intervention and control or comparison groups in the study is the level of the independent variable administered. When other systematic and important differences exist between groups, we refer to this as selection bias. Probability suggests that by randomly allocating participants to the groups in the study, the important characteristics of participants (characteristics that are likely to impact on the findings) will be more or less evenly distributed between groups – hence the desirability of the randomised controlled trial. Yet this 'even-ing-out' of groups on the basis of probability is likely to be true in cases only where your sample size is large (as probability refers to the likelihood of events 'in the long run'). Alternative strategies to achieve an approximate even distribution of important characteristics (which might influence the study outcomes) among groups with small sample sizes include stratified randomisation and minimisation.

Stratified randomisation means conducting randomisation within each subgroup of interest. For example, suppose you are conducting a randomised controlled trial of an intervention to encourage exercise uptake among people with diabetes. You want to ensure that the distribution of people with a normal body mass index and people who are classified as overweight is similar in the intervention group and the control group. (A classification of weight status might be a bit more sensitive than this in reality, but for the purposes of the example I want to keep it simple.) These subgroups (normal weight and overweight) are referred to as strata (plural of stratum). In stratified randomisation, you would construct a randomisation list for each stratum (subgroup). That is, a randomisation list for overweight individuals and a randomisation list for normal weight individuals. Stratified randomisation works when there are a small number of strata (in relation to the sample size). When you wish to take account of several variables, and hence many strata when using a small sample size, then minimisation should be considered.

Minimisation is a procedure for allocating participants to groups on the basis of minimising the differences between groups on important characteristics (characteristics which are hypothesised to impact on the outcomes). In other words, the group that a participant is allocated to depends on the characteristics of the people already allocated to groups.

There are different strategies for conducting allocation by minimisation, and a random element to the allocation procedure can be introduced. Therefore, software specifically designed for the purpose should be considered (see Altman & Bland, 2005).

Often, randomly allocating participants to study groups is not possible or is not acceptable for ethical reasons. In these situations, there should be some consideration about the choice of a comparison or control group and its effect on the conclusions of the study. For example, in health-related research, a 'waiting-list control group' is often used. In effect this means that people who have been on a waiting list and are next in line for treatment will receive the intervention and those who remain on the waiting list will be used as a control group. This is often a popular choice because it provides a form of engagement for those on the waiting list (so they feel that they have not been forgotten), and it avoids the ethical dilemma of whom to allocate to the treatment group (although it can raise other ethical dilemmas about people on the waiting list agreeing to participate in the research in the false belief that this means their progress through the waiting list will be hastened). Before choosing this relatively convenient option, it is important to consider how this might affect your conclusions. In other words, what are the differences between those receiving the intervention and those on the waiting list? At the very least, those on the waiting list are likely to have been waiting for a shorter period of time for treatment than those now receiving the intervention. If the waiting time for treatment in the service is long, then the differences between the waiting list control group and the intervention group could be substantial and might be important if there is a correlation between waiting time and health status.

An alternative to randomly allocating participants or using minimisation is to develop a control group using matched pairs. This means that for everyone who enters the intervention group, someone enters the control group who matches the intervention group participant on all relevant characteristics. This is a powerful research design, as the matched pairs design can be treated like a within-subjects design, but it is rare to find in practice, given the logistical difficulties of finding a match for every participant.

4.1.1.8   Regression to the mean

This refers to the tendency of extreme scores to move closer to the mean score at later data collection points. For example, if participants are chosen to take part in a study because they have an extreme score on the outcome measure at baseline, then it is likely that this score will become less extreme over time. The presence of a control or comparison group, where participants begin with equally extreme scores as those in the intervention group, will help to distinguish the effects of the intervention from this statistical artefact.

4.1.1.9 Mere measurement

Completing the outcome measures might in itself be a form of an intervention in that it might cause the participant to consider the issues presented to them in the outcome measures and reflect on them, thereby resulting in different responses at a second administration of the same measures. Given that repeated testing is an important element of evaluating interventions, this is a strong potential threat to internal validity. Of course, we can balance the effects of any pre-test by also including a pre-test for a control or comparison group but that does not allow us to estimate the true effect of the intervention. To address this problem, you should consider using a Solomon 4 group design. In this design, there are two control groups and two intervention groups. One of the control groups and one of the intervention groups receives a pre-test and a post-test (the classic experimental design); the other control group and intervention group receive the post-test but no pre-test. In this way, the effects of the intervention and the effects of completing the pre-test can be isolated and estimated.

The difficulty with the Solomon 4 group design is that it requires a larger sample size than a classic two-group experimental design.

4.1.1.10 Intervention fidelity

When an intervention is delivered on more than one occasion, that is to more than one group or individual, and/or when an intervention is delivered separately by more than one interventionist, then we need to consider whether the intervention will be delivered in the same way each time. For example, in the cardiac rehabilitation study discussed in Section 4.1.1.2, the intervention was delivered separately by two psychologists, due to time constraints. As we knew that we wanted to combine the results from the intervention sessions conducted by both psychologists, we needed to make sure in advance that both psychologists were following a standard approach to delivering the intervention. Of course, this does not account for the differences in interpersonal style, which is an important element of a one-to-one talking therapy type of intervention, but ongoing checks during the course of the research helped to ensure that at least the form of the intervention was similar across the two psychologists.

4.1.1.11 Construct validity

Some authors will make a distinction between internal validity and construct validity. (I have not done up to this point, and some of the threats to internal validity mentioned above are also threats to construct validity.) Whereas internal validity is the extent to which you can make cause-and-effect conclusions, construct validity refers to why these cause and effect relationships have been found. To a large extent, construct validity asks about the effective ingredients of the intervention – what is it about the intervention that caused the observed effect? In some cases, this may be the method of delivery of the intervention, or it might be the interventionist (and if the intervention was delivered by someone else, then it would not be as effective), or, in the case of a talking therapy intervention, it might be simply that the participant was being attended to rather than any specific therapeutic approach of the intervention. Of course, it is useful just to know that an intervention is effective, but if we want to be able to recommend the intervention, then we also need to know why it is effective. Sometimes it is not possible to answer both questions in a single research study and a series of studies may be required to tease out the effective ingredients of the intervention. However, the more you can build in procedures which allow you to say something about the effective ingredients, the higher quality your research design will be.

4.1.2 How can I maximise external validity in my study design?

External validity is often separated into ecological validity and population validity. Ecological validity refers to the extent to which the research procedures are unobtrusive and/or natural, thereby assessing participant responses in a non-artificial setting. Population validity is the extent to which the findings from the research are likely to be generalisable to the wider population – in other words, the extent to which the study sample represents the study population. Given the emphasis on control and manipulation to achieve high internal validity and the emphasis on non-artificiality to achieve high external validity, it is not surprising that there is sometimes a tension between maximising internal validity and external validity. In these situations, you need to make a judgement about which type of validity should be prioritised, on the basis of the aims of the study. Consequently, when testing an intervention under controlled, potentially artificial settings, we refer to the efficacy of an intervention, and when testing an intervention in a more natural field setting, we refer to the effectiveness of an intervention.

Usually, an assessment of population validity, or the extent to which your study sample is a good representation of the population of interest, is based on the type of sampling used. Although the definition of the population of interest will also limit the generalisability of your findings, it is better to have a representative sample of a small population than a non-representative sample of a large population. In the former case, you will be able to generalise your findings to your small population with confidence, thereby allowing you to draw strong conclusions, albeit about a relatively small group of people. In the latter case, you will not be clear about whom your findings apply to. Therefore, to enhance population validity, you should be concerned about the sampling procedures specified in your research proposal. That said, it is important to recognise that the more limited your population of interest is, the more limited you research will be in terms of its usefulness to other people. The training requirements of health and clinical psychology require you to produce research which is of a standard that could be suitable for publication in a peer-reviewed academic journal. These journals will not want to publish research which does not interest a reasonably wide range of readers.

In broad terms, your sampling strategy will either be based on probability or not based on probability. For quantitative research, probability-based sampling strategies are best as they result in a sample for which we can make reasonable assumptions about representativeness. In probability-based sampling, every member of the population has a known, non-zero chance of being selected for the sample (this implies random selection). In non-probability-based sampling, some members of the population have a chance of being selected for the study and others do not. The most common forms of probability-based sampling are

- *Simple random sample.* In a simple random sample, everyone in the population has an equal chance of being selected for the sample. Basically, the name of everyone in the population is put in a hat and the number of people required for the sample is drawn out of the hat at random (of course, computers are used to do this more efficiently than names in a hat!). The list of everyone in the population is known as the sampling frame.
- *Stratified sample.* A stratified sample is used when we want to ensure that our sample contains specified proportions of people with certain characteristics. For example, we might want to ensure that our sample contains a proportion of males and females similar to that found in the population, as we believe that being male or female will have an important impact on the results from the study and we don't want one group to be over or under represented. Consequently, we divide our sampling frame into males and females (known as strata) and then take a random sample of the appropriate number

from each. In the long run, a simple random sample would achieve the same result, but if we are using a small sample then stratification is a useful strategy. A stratified sample is also used to obtain samples which are disproportionate to the population (most often found in large scale surveys where the variance of the target variables is known to vary across strata – not the type of research a trainee psychologist is likely to engage in).

- *Multistage cluster sample.* Cluster sampling is used to avoid the high costs of interviewing participants who are spread over a large geographical area. It is, therefore, inappropriate for surveys where interviews are conducted over a small geographical area or for surveys which use postal questionnaires or telephone interviewing. However, multistage cluster sampling is useful in situations where the complete sampling frame is unknown. The process first involves selecting clusters of people. These clusters are naturally occurring units such as election wards, GP surgeries and so on, and they can be selected with probability proportionate to their size, to account for the size differences between clusters. At the next stage, a further random sample of smaller units (perhaps individuals) is taken from these clusters. Multistage cluster sampling appears to be an efficient approach to sampling, but it must be noted that the efficiency of the method decreases as homogeneity within the cluster increases.

In many situations, it is difficult to obtain a probability-based sample, because it is difficult, if not impossible, to obtain a full or partial sampling frame. Therefore, non-probability-based sampling is often found in psychological research. The type of non-probability sampling strategy used will depend on the nature of the research, and its choice should be justified in your research proposal. Some common types of non-probability-based sampling are

- *Snowball sampling.* This is where you identify a member of the population of interest, and they introduce you to other members of the population, and so on, so that your sample is added to by the people recruited for the study. This is a useful approach when the population of interest is rare or secretive, and therefore it is extremely difficult for someone from the 'outside' to be able to identify potential research participants.
- *Quota sampling.* This is similar to stratified sampling, but without the randomness. Let's take the example referred to under the discussion of stratified sampling, where we want specified proportions of males

and females in our sample. In quota sampling, we would set quotas for the recruitment of males and females. For example, we might state that we need 40 males and 60 females. In practice, when we reached the quota for males, we would not recruit any more males into the sample but continue to recruit females (or vice versa).

- *Convenience sampling.* This is the least stringent and, unfortunately, the most common type of sampling strategy. In convenience sampling we recruit participants into our sample because they are easy to access. In psychological research this often means undergraduate psychology students. In applied health-related psychological research this often means the people who turn up at an outpatients' clinic on a specific day. Sometimes we have no choice than to conduct some form of convenience sampling, but some effort should be made to try to reduce any sampling bias where possible. For example, deciding a priori to recruit consecutive attendees at an outpatients' clinic on a range of dates would help to address the charge that participants were being hand-picked to provide you with the results you desired or that the findings are restricted to people who attended the clinic on one day.

Apart from the sampling strategy used, population validity is threatened by small sample sizes and high rates of attrition. In general terms, the larger the sample size, the more likely it is that you have a sample which represents all the sectors of your population. Additionally, there is no point in going to the trouble of obtaining a representative sample if a considerable proportion of the sample do not complete the study, resulting in a final data set which is based on an unrepresentative sample. Attrition has been highlighted previously as a threat to internal validity, and, therefore, including procedures which will minimise attrition in your research proposal is very important.

4.2 Choosing a data collection instrument

A major component of a research proposal is the justification for the choice of data collection method. The quality of the data collected, and, therefore, the conclusions that can be drawn from your analyses, are largely influenced by the data collection method. Indeed, it could be considered unethical to involve people in a study without being reasonably confident that the data they provide will be useful in addressing the research question. Therefore, the rationale for your choice of data collection method will need to be made explicit.

This is particularly important in psychological research. The psychological constructs that we are often interested in are usually not directly measurable. Therefore, we have developed approaches and instruments which provide us with indicators of these psychological constructs. As a result, there is an onus on a researcher to argue that their chosen method is appropriate for the proposed research.

4.2.1   How do I justify my choice of questionnaires/tests?

Most psychological constructs assessed by questionnaires/tests cannot be measured directly. The questionnaires and tests are an attempt to provide an indication of the psychological construct of interest. Therefore, it is important to ensure that the questionnaire/test you choose is likely to provide an observed score which is a good representation of the true score for the construct of interest. In other words, you need to demonstrate that your chosen instrument has evidence for reliability and validity. In addition to these properties, you might want to consider the sensitivity of the instrument, the burden on participants created by completing the instrument and the extent to which the instrument is understandable by your target population.

4.2.1.1   Reliability

Reliability indices of any questionnaires/tests to be used in your proposed research should be presented in your proposal. The reliability of an instrument refers to its stability. This can mean stability over time (the extent to which you would obtain similar results in repeated administration of the test) or internal stability (the extent to which the items within the instrument are related to each other). What unites the different forms of reliability is that they are based on the amount of error in the measurement.

Measurement error comes in two forms: systematic (where the error is consistent) and unsystematic (where the error is random). We attempt to counteract systematic errors by carefully writing items on a test and presenting them in a different format, such as ensuring that half the items on a questionnaire are reverse scored. We attempt to counteract unsystematic errors by constructing tests with many items (working on the assumption that random errors will cancel each other out in the long run). The reliability of a test is an indicator of the extent to which the test is affected by unsystematic (random) error. The higher the reliability, the less the test has been affected by random error.

One of the most commonly used indices of reliability is Cronbach's Alpha (α), which provides a reliability index between zero and one, with a score closer to one indicating higher reliability. Cronbach's alpha tells us the extent to which observed scores on the test are consistent with (or correlate with) true scores. On the basis that the observed score on a test is made up of the true score on the test and random error, as random error decreases (reliability increases), the observed score will reflect more closely the true score. In fact, with very large samples, the square root of Cronbach's alpha will provide a close estimate of the correlation coefficient between a true score and an observed score. However, this measure of consistency has limited value, and it might be more useful to calculate the discrepancy between the observed score and the true score.

The standard error of measurement (SEM) indicates how close an observed score is likely to be to a true score. The SEM can be calculated by taking the square root of 1 minus Cronbach's alpha and then multiplying the result by the standard deviation of the test ($SEM = SD\sqrt{1-\alpha}$). When we have calculated the SEM, we can then say that there is a 95 % chance that a person's true score on a test will lie within ±1.96 SEMs of their observed score. The SEM is particularly important when we are using instruments as part of our assessment of individuals, and we wish to compare the person's score with another score (such as a norm value or a fixed cut-off point, or the person's score at a previous point in time to chart progress). It is of less concern when we are using group summary scores from a test, as is often the case in quantitative research projects.

An additional method of assessing reliability is the test-retest method. This is not an alternative to an assessment of internal consistency (as provided by Cronbach's alpha), as it provides information about a different property of the measurement instrument. Therefore, the evidence supporting your choice of a test will be stronger if you report estimates of internal consistency and test-retest reliability. Test-retest reliability is calculated by administering the test at two points in time and then comparing the results. The more reliable the test, the more similar the two results will be. The difficulty with the test-retest method is choosing an appropriate time delay between testing to ensure that it is not too short (in which case problems like practice effects may impact on the results) or that it is not too long (during which time people may change on the construct of interest). Test-retest reliability is estimated by calculating a correlation coefficient (to assess the consistency of the results) or an intra-class correlation coefficient (to assess the similarity of the results). See Box 4.1 for a description of the intra-class correlation coefficient. In both cases, the index provided ranges from 0 to 1, with a score closer to 1 indicating higher reliability. The intra-class correlation coefficient is also a useful statistic in assessing inter-rater reliability in situations where an observation schedule is the data collection instrument.

Box 4.1   The intra-class correlation coefficient

The intra-class correlation coefficient (ICC) is a statistic which assesses agreement between raters or among scores on a variable assessed at different points in time (as in the case of test-retest reliability). Therefore, the ICC is used in circumstances similar to weighted kappa (see Box 2.1), however, the ICC can be used for continuous data and with more than two raters (or time points). The ICC is based on the principle that if scores are similar across time (or similar across raters), then the variability within scores from a case (e.g. pair of scores) should constitute a considerably smaller proportion of the total variability than the variability between cases. The ICC is calculated as follows:

$$ICC = \frac{SD_b^2 - SD_w^2}{SD_b^2 + SD_w^2}$$

where

SD_b^2 = standard deviation between subjects (e.g. variability between each pair of scores),

SD_w^2 = standard deviation within subject (e.g. variability within each pair of scores)

Usually, these SD values are calculated from the results of a one-way ANOVA, where the time points (or raters) are designated as the independent variable and the scores on the test are the dependent variable. The ICC can then be calculated using the equation above where the SD values are the mean square (MS) values obtained in the ANOVA table.

4.2.1.2   Validity

When an instrument is valid, it means that it measures what it claims to measure. Presenting evidence for the validity of a questionnaire/test is essential in your research proposal. There are three things to remember about this. Firstly, when assessing psychological constructs we cannot say that a test is either valid or not valid, as we do not have a direct measure of the construct against which the performance of our test can be gauged. Therefore, we can only present evidence for the validity of our instrument. The more evidence we can present and the stronger this evidence is, the more we will convince our reader that the instrument we have chosen is likely to be valid. Secondly, validity is population specific. That is, just because there is evidence for the validity of an instrument in one population, it does not follow that the instrument is likely to be valid in other populations. The evidence for validity that you present in your proposal should be specific to your population of interest if possible. Thirdly, we should probably refer to 'validities' rather than 'validity', as there is more than one type of validity. The validities that will be most convincing for the readers of your research proposal are criterion validity and construct validity.

The level of criterion validity of an instrument refers to the extent to which the instrument relates to a specified criterion measure in the way that we would expect. There are two types of criterion validity: concurrent validity and predictive validity. In concurrent validity, the instrument under investigation is administered at the same time as the criterion measure. In predictive validity, the criterion measure is administered at some time after the instrument of interest. In this case, the criterion is a known ('gold standard') assessment of the psychological construct of interest. Evidence for criterion validity is provided by strong correlations between the instrument and the criterion measure. For example, the 'gold standard' assessment of dietary fat intake is considered to be a biomarker such as triglyceride levels, obtained from a blood test. However, such a test is costly and requires access to the appropriate resources. Therefore, food frequency questionnaires have been developed to obtain self-report information about dietary behaviour, which can then be converted to an estimate of fat intake. For a food frequency questionnaire to be considered to have good evidence for criterion validity, the estimates of fat intake derived from the questionnaire would need to correlate strongly with a biomarker such as triglyceride levels.

Construct validity can be considered to take three different types: convergent validity, divergent validity and structural validity. Convergent validity is demonstrated when the instrument relates to similar theoretical constructs in the way that it should. A particular form of convergent validity is discriminant validity. This is shown when the instrument can discriminate between groups of people in the way that it should. For example, if your instrument purports to measure anxiety, then it should correlate (moderately) with scores on a measure of depression (as depression and anxiety are usually found to correlate at least moderate–strongly). This would be evidence for convergent validity. Alternatively, you could show that your instrument can discriminate (to some extent) between people with a diagnosis of depression and those without a diagnosis of depression, which would provide evidence for discriminant validity. However, you would also want to show that your instrument did not correlate very strongly with a measure of depression; otherwise, it might lead you to wonder whether your instrument was actually measuring depression rather than anxiety. Evidence which demonstrates that your instrument is distinct from measures of other constructs is referred to as divergent validity.

Structural validity refers to the validity of the proposed structure of the instrument. For example, many questionnaires are divided into subscales, and the questionnaire information will tell you which items constitute the different subscales. An assessment of structural validity is an assessment of whether the questionnaire should be divided into subscales (that is, whether the subscales are sufficiently distinct) and whether there is evidence to support the proposed allocation of items to subscales. Evidence for structural validity is usually provided in the form of a factor analysis (see Tabachnick & Fidell, 2007, chapters 13 and 14 for a discussion of factor analysis).

4.2.1.3 Sensitivity

The sensitivity (or responsiveness) of an instrument is an important property to consider (and include in your proposal) when you intend to use the instrument to assess change. For example, if you are proposing to evaluate an intervention as part of your research, you will wish to assess the outcome of interest before and after the intervention, with some expectation that the intervention will cause a change on this outcome. However, if the assessment instrument you use to measure the outcome is not sensitive to change, then it might not be able to reveal the important changes that have resulted from the intervention. Consequently, someone reading your research proposal will want to be reassured that the instrument you have chosen will be appropriate for this purpose.

Sensitivity of an instrument is usually demonstrated by an effect size statistic (see Section 2.4). The common effect sizes provided take the form of the change in mean scores on the instrument divided by a standard deviation. In some cases, this standard deviation is taken to be the standard deviation of the baseline scores and in other cases this is the standard deviation of the change scores. When the latter is used, the effect size is known as the standardised response mean. In either case, values up to 0.5 are considered small; values between 0.5 and 0.8 are considered moderate; and values greater than 0.8 are considered large (McDowell, 2006, p. 38).

4.2.1.4 Burden/feasibility

In addition to including information about reliability, validity and (where appropriate) sensitivity in your research proposal, it is helpful to include some information about other characteristics of your chosen instruments, to further strengthen your case for their selection. Issues that you might consider are

- Is the wording culturally appropriate?
- Is the wording likely to be understood by the research population? For example, is it designed for adults but you intend to use it with children or is the wording too complicated?
- Is the length of the questionnaire/test likely to be burdensome for participants?
- Will the questionnaire need to be translated for some participants?

Some of these issues can be readily addressed by demonstrating that the chosen instrument has been used in a similar population in previous research with success (that is, with a high response rate, low proportion of missing items and so on).

4.2.2   Can I construct my own questionnaire?

When you intend to use a questionnaire to collect quantitative data that provides an indicator of a psychological construct, then it is probably not a good idea to construct your own questionnaire as part of a research study. As we have just seen, these types of instruments need to be justified with a substantial amount of information, and this information is often provided across more than one study. Therefore, trying to develop your own questionnaire as part of a study is probably unrealistic during your training programme. However, it may be feasible and appropriate for you to propose a research study which is devoted to the development and testing of a questionnaire. If you wish to do this, then a useful guideline for the type of evidence you need to generate is provided by COSMIN (COnsensus-based Standards for the selection of health status Measurement INstruments) (Mokkink et al., 2010).

There are a few exceptions to this suggestion. Sometimes, in psychological research, you will need to create a situation-specific version of a questionnaire. A common example of this is when you are assessing the constructs of the Theory of Planned Behaviour (Ajzen, 1985), which is a theory of cognitive determinants of health behaviour. There is no single questionnaire that assesses these constructs, as each questionnaire needs to be specific to the health behaviour under investigation. However, a suggested questionnaire structure and a set of guidelines exist for the construction of an appropriate questionnaire (http://people.umass.edu/aizen/tpb.html). Therefore, it might be appropriate to adapt existing questionnaires or questionnaire structures for your own purposes, in the presence of tried and tested methods for doing so.

4.3 Small n experiments

A special type of design used in quantitative research is the experimental design conducted with single cases or a small number of cases. These are often known as small n experiments (where the n refers to the sample size). It is worth singling out this type of experimental design for special consideration as this design is not unusual in health and clinical psychology research.

4.3.1 How do I design a small n experiment?

The design of a small n experiment is usually referred to by the number of phases that a participant experiences. The A phase of the experiment is the phase during which data are collected about the participant but no treatment or intervention is provided. The B phase is the phase during which data are collected and the intervention is in place. We talk about phases of the experiment because the phase is usually a period which contains several data collection points, rather than a single point in time with a single data collection point. Indeed, it is the repeated data collection at each phase of the experiment and the alternating phases of the experiment that makes up for the lack of a control or comparison group. It is the pattern of results which lends support to our conclusions with more confidence than we could place on single data collection points.

The most basic of all small n experiments is the ABA design. In this design, the first A phase is the baseline phase. In all small n experiments, it is necessary to demonstrate a stable baseline before moving to the B phase. A stable baseline is demonstrated by showing that the outcome of interest remains stable over several repeated measurements during this phase. If the intervention is effective, then the outcome measures should change in a clinically important way during the B phase, and this change should be at least maintained across repeated measurements during this phase. To provide further support to the conclusion that it was the intervention that caused the change and not some extraneous variable, the experiment then returns to another A phase (the intervention is removed) and the results on the outcome measure should change from that found during the B phase, perhaps returning to the levels found during the first A phase.

The ABA design can sometimes raise an ethical dilemma – we have just demonstrated that an intervention is effective, but we have removed the intervention from the participant for the purposes of the research. Therefore, we might wish to employ an ABAB design, where a final phase is added which reinstates the intervention. In fact, if the changes in the outcome measure detected during the first B phase are found again during the second B phase, this design will provide even stronger evidence of the effect of the intervention than the ABA design, so there is more than one reason for favouring the ABAB approach.

The difficulty with using either an ABA or ABAB design is that it might not be possible to remove the effects of the intervention. For example, if the purpose of the intervention is to help an individual to learn a new skill, then it could be impossible to remove this effect – to make the person 'un-learn' the skill. In this situation, you should consider using a multiple baseline design. Effectively, a multiple baseline design follows an AB design, but comparators are included to account for the lack of ability to alternate phases. This type of design is similar to an interrupted time series design with controls.

A common type of multiple baseline design is multiple baseline across cases. In this situation, you have more than one participant in your study, and the intervention is administered to each participant at a different time. If the intervention affects only the individual to whom it is targeted at that point in time, then this can help to eliminate the possibility that extraneous variables are causing the observed effect. In Figure 4.1, three participants are included in the study. For Person 3, the baseline phase ends at the fifth data collection point, and you can see the increase in scores as the intervention is introduced at this point. However, the scores of the remaining participants remain steady until they are provided with the intervention in turn (after point seven for Person 2 and after point nine for Person 1).

Small n experiments can appear to be an easy way of conducting research without the requirement of recruiting a large number of participants. However, it is important to reiterate that although you will not need to recruit a large sample size when conducting this type of experiment, you will need to collect data on the participants at many time points. This means that your data collection will take time, and there is also a high risk of someone dropping out of your study. While the odd dropout from a large group of participants is usually not crucial, in small n experiments, it could mean that all data collected up to that point are wasted and the experiment will need to begin again. Additionally, sometimes it is difficult to predict how long it will take before you obtain a stable baseline and, therefore, when you can introduce the intervention.

It may be that withholding the intervention until this happens is unacceptable for the well-being of the participant, so the opportunity for the research disappears. Like any good quality research, there will be obstacles to the implementation of this type of research design, so its feasibility and the availability of a back-up plan should be given careful consideration.

4.3.2 How do I analyse data collected in a small n experiment?

It is possible that a small n experiment will give you the opportunity to collect qualitative as well as quantitative data. The analysis of qualitative data is addressed in Chapter 6. In this section, I aim to focus on the approach to analysing the quantitative data obtained using this type of design.

A useful first step in the analysis of data obtained from small n experiments is to plot the data on a graph, similar to that in Figure 4.1. This will help to identify any patterns in the data and any obvious effects of the intervention. In fact, some researchers are happy to limit their analysis to this approach. However, sometimes the effects of an intervention are not as dramatic or obvious as that suggested by Figure 4.1, and you might wish to enlist the help of some statistical procedures. A simple approach is to calculate the mean score on the outcome measure for each phase of the experiment and then compare the means. You might want to take this a step further and use a formal statistical test to compare the mean scores at each phase, using an ANOVA, for example. The problem

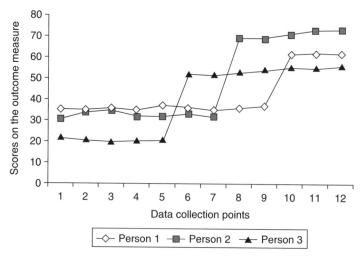

Figure 4.1 Multiple baseline across cases

with using a test such as this is that it assumes that the scores in the analysis are independent, whereas the scores in your analysis are obtained from a single participant and, therefore, are clearly not independent. Alternative statistical tests have been developed to deal with this situation (see Todman & Dugard, 2001; Bulté & Onghena, 2009).

5

Analysing Quantitative Data

●●

I think it is fair to say that statistics is not the topic that undergraduate psychology students enjoy most. It is often treated as a necessary evil – something that students will study just enough to enable them to do the analysis they need to do and then instantly forget (with some relief). Those charged with teaching the subject can easily become frustrated with this apparent lack of interest, motivation and willingness to engage that is demonstrated by the students. Of course, trainee psychologists are a different story. Trainee psychologists have chosen to pursue a career in psychology, they understand the importance and relevance of data analysis skills, and they are keen to develop in ways that will enable them to contribute to research knowledge in their chosen profession – aren't you?? Unfortunately, that might not be true, and the attitudes about statistics that you developed as an undergraduate student are likely to be the same as the attitudes you have now. I can understand this, and I think I know what the problem is. I have seen eager trainees attending their first statistics class of their postgraduate training with a new-found motivation to pay attention to everything that is being said and then losing the will to stay awake after about 30 minutes of a discussion on hypothetical distributions. I know that other demands are being made on your time and clearing a space to spend the time to truly understand statistical analysis is very difficult. I know that this results in you taking a more pragmatic ('what do I need to know') approach to conducting statistical analysis and that can often result in a little resentment about the expectations placed on you ('I want to be a psychologist, not a statistician'). So I know that what you really want is a concise guide to conducting statistical analysis, free from the hypothetical discussions – something that will help you perform the analysis you need to and provide you with a basic understanding of what you are doing. This is what I aim to provide in this chapter.

Writing this chapter is not easy for me. I am a statistician, and there are lots of things that I want to write about statistics because I find them interesting (believe it or not!). There are also lots of things I want to write about because I genuinely believe that they are useful bits of information – maybe not immediately but perhaps at some time in your future. Furthermore, by omitting the theoretical discussions surrounding statistics I am likely to be ridiculed by any other statistician who happens to read this book! In my defence, my rationale for the content of this chapter is

1. I could spend a considerable amount of time writing about the bits of statistics that I would like you to understand, but I know most of you will skip over.
2. There are several good books already written which provide a more in-depth discussion of statistical analysis (for example, Greer & Mulhern, 2011).
3. I have slowly come to the realisation that not everyone who uses statistics needs to understand everything about statistics. Perhaps it is appropriate to aim for different levels of understanding for different purposes, with the caveat that you are aware of the limitation in your knowledge. I like the analogy of owning a car. I can carry out some routine maintenance of my car (for example, change a wheel, check tyre pressure, top-up the oil, change a wiper blade), but I can't do any more in-depth work (for example, replace the brake pads, fit a new exhaust pipe, replace the fuel pump). In fact, I'm not really sure how a car engine works, but does that mean I should not be allowed to drive one? The important thing is that when the car makes a funny noise or a strange light starts flashing, I take it to a car mechanic. In other words, my limited knowledge is sufficient some of the time, but I know my knowledge is limited, and I seek help when I need it. This chapter is based on the same premise – it aims to provide you with a limited, working knowledge of statistics on the assumption that you will seek help as and when appropriate.

5.1 Getting help

Given that the material in this chapter is meant to be a basic guide, built on the assumption that you will get help when you need it, it seems appropriate to first address questions relevant to this premise.

5.1.1   When should I get help?

If you have already collected your data and you then approach a statistics advisor to assist with conducting your analysis, you have left it much
too late, and there will be a limit to how much the statistics advisor will
be able to help you. I strongly encourage those who are embarking on
a quantitative research project and who do not have a very good grasp
of statistics to involve a statistics advisor in your research team from the
outset. This person will provide useful advice about sample size calculations and the type of data that you should collect in order to answer
your research questions. Furthermore, if your statistics advisor has not
been involved in the project from the outset, then they will not be familiar with the rationale for the study and, therefore, will not be able to
advise on alternative data analysis strategies which might be useful for
your research project. Instead, the statistics advisor will simply answer
the questions you ask (which puts the onus on you to ask the correct
questions).

I have purposely referred to a statistics advisor rather than a statistician as you can get good advice from a psychologist with an interest and
extensive experience in statistical analysis as well as from someone who
is a chartered statistician.

5.1.2   What should I expect when I meet with a statistics advisor?

The guiding principle is that the statistics advisor should be there to provide advice and guidance, not to conduct your statistical analysis for you.
Therefore, I think that a good general model is that you use a statistics
advisor to check your thoughts on the approach to your analysis rather
than expecting this person to develop plan of analysis for you. In summary, if you meet with your statistics advisor and say something like
'here is my data and my research questions; how should I analyse the
data?' then you are expecting too much. In addition, your lack of input
into the consideration of the analysis will be obvious to any assessors of
your research in a viva exam (and/or in your project report). Although
your assessors will not expect to hear you speak/write about your analysis
like a statistician, they will expect you to demonstrate that your analysis
plan was considered by you. So a better approach would be to meet with
your statistics advisor and say something like 'here are my data and my
research questions. I think that I should analyse the data in the following
way…do you think this is appropriate?'

Additionally, your statistics advisor will probably expect that you have
'cleaned' your data before asking him/her to look at it. By cleaning your

data I mean that you should make sure that there are no erroneous scores in your data set. Most often this happens when you do a double key tap when entering data. For example, you enter a score of 66 instead of 6. So careful scrutiny of your data set is needed before progressing to the analysis phase. This can be done in many ways, the simplest of which is to run frequency tables for each variable in your data set and examine the frequency tables to see whether there are any values which should not be there because they are out of the possible range of scores.

When you are sure that your data set is clean, you should also consider how you want to handle any missing values. There are a number of strategies for doing this. If you are not sure how to manage missing values, then you might want to arrange an appointment with your statistics advisor to discuss this issue before moving to the analysis stage (also see Section 5.3.4).

You should also consider whether variables in your data set need to be recoded and/or whether variables need to be combined to create scale scores. These tasks do not require statistical expertise, but a good understanding of the data collection instruments you have used, a good working knowledge of your data management software (such as SPSS) and some time. Therefore, you should not expect your statistics advisor to do them for you.

Also, it will be beneficial to generate some descriptive statistics (such as means and standard deviations) for the variables in your data set.

Finally, when you have obtained advice from your statistics advisor, you should be prepared to run the analysis by yourself. There are many guides which provide step-by-step instructions to conducting statistical analyses within a range of software packages (for example, Brace, Kemp & Snelgar, 2009).

5.2   Common statistical tests

This section aims to provide you with a guide to the choice of commonly used statistical tests. It is important to bear in mind that this is not an exhaustive list of statistical tests. There might be other tests which are more suited to the type of analysis needed for your project – hence the value of having a statistics advisor. The purpose of this section is to provide a pointer to the types of statistical tests you might want to read about in more depth. This is not meant to be a comprehensive guide to using these tests, and I would strongly recommend that you obtain a good statistics book to help you with your analyses (for example, Brace et al., 2009; Greer & Mulhern, 2001).

5.2.1   How do I examine relationships/associations/ differences between two variables?

Sometimes your research questions will be concerned simply with two variables, although often your research will be more complex than this. Examples of research questions that focus on two variables are:

- What is the relationship between self-efficacy and frequency of exercise?
- What is the difference between the level of depressive symptoms reported by adults who have experienced trauma in childhood and the level of depressive symptoms reported by adults who have not experienced trauma in childhood?
- What is the association between smoking and binge drinking?

The choice of an appropriate statistical test to answer these questions depends on how the variables are measured (whether the data are categorical or continuous) and the shape of the data (whether the data are skewed or approximately normal). I will return to a discussion about the shape of the data in Section 5.3. When a categorical variable is one of the variables in the analysis, the choice of appropriate test is also determined by the number of categories within this variable. Table 5.1 provides a guide to the test most likely to be appropriate for your analysis when both variables in your analysis are categorical. Some of these tests might be unfamiliar to you, so the following (read in conjunction with Table 5.1) provides a brief guide to when they should be used:

- McNemar – used when examining related scores (for example, change over two points in time) on a dichotomous variable.
- Tetrachoric correlation coefficient – a correlation coefficient generated when both variables are dichotomous but are assumed to represent an underlying normal distribution.
- Chi-square – used to examine the association between two categorical variables. The chi-square statistic provides no indication of the strength of the association – it is a point on a distribution which enables you to determine the statistical significance of the association. All other things being held constant, chi-square will increase as the sample size increases.
- Phi/Cramer's V – a measure of strength of the association between two categorical variables, which is based on chi-square but takes account of the sample size.

Table 5.1 Choosing a test to examine relationships between two categorical variables

Outcome/Criterion/ Dependent variable	Predictor/Independent variable	Possible statistics
2 categories	2 categories	McNemar Tetrachoric correlation coefficient Chi-square Phi Odds ratio
2 categories	> 2 categories	Cochran's Q Chi-square Cramer's V
> 2 categories	2 categories	Chi-square Cramer's V Mann-Whitney U Wilcoxon Matched Pairs
> 2 categories	> 2 categories	Chi-square Cramer's V Polychoric correlation coefficient Spearman's rho correlation coefficient Kruskal-Wallis Friedman

Note: When bivariate correlation coefficients are conducted, we do not need to specify which is the independent variable and which is the dependent variable.

- Odds Ratio – used to compare the odds of an event occurring in one group with the odds of this event occurring in another group. In this case, the 'event' is the occurrence of one of two possible outcomes.
- Cochran's Q – used when examining related scores from more than two points (for example, scores from three or more points in time) on a dichotomous variable.
- Mann-Whitney U – examines differences between two groups on a dependent variable measured at the ordinal level (at least).
- Wilcoxon matched pairs – examines differences between two related points (for example, two points in time) on a dependent variable measured at the ordinal level (at least).
- Polychoric correlation coefficient – a correlation coefficient generated when both variables are measured at the ordinal level but are assumed to represent an underlying normal distribution.
- Spearman's rho correlation coefficient – a correlation coefficient generated when both variables are measured at the ordinal level (at least)
- Kruskal-Wallis – examines differences among two or more groups on a dependent variable measured at the ordinal level (at least).

- Friedman – examines differences among two or more related points (for example, three points in time) on a dependent variable measured at the ordinal level (at least).

When at least one variable in your analysis is continuous, we must consider a different set of statistical tests (see Table 5.2).

Many of the tests listed in Table 5.2 should be familiar to you. However, a brief guide follows:

- Independent t-test – used when the categories on the independent variable are not related (for example, two separate groups), when variances of the two groups are approximately equal (although some statistical software will provide a correction for this) and when a normal distribution is assumed. When any of the final two conditions cannot be met, the Mann-Whitney U test can be used.
- Paired t-test – used when the categories on the independent variable are related (for example, scores obtained at two points in time) and when a normal distribution is assumed. When the final condition cannot be met, the Wilcoxon Matched Pairs test can be used.

Table 5.2 Choosing a test to examine relationships between two variables (where at least one is continuous)

Outcome/Criterion/ Dependent variable	Predictor/Independent variable	Possible statistics
Continuous	2 categories	Independent t-test Paired t-test Mann-Whitney U Wilcoxon Matched Pairs Point biserial correlation coefficient Biserial correlation coefficient
Continuous	> 2 categories	One-way ANOVA Repeated measures ANOVA Kruskal-Wallis Friedman Polyserial correlation coefficient Spearman's rho correlation coefficient
2 categories	Continuous	Point biserial correlation coefficient Biserial correlation coefficient
> 2 categories	Continuous	Polyserial correlation coefficient Spearman's rho correlation coefficient
Continuous	Continuous	Spearman's rho correlation coefficient Pearson's r correlation coefficient

Note: When bivariate correlation coefficients are conducted, we do not need to specify which is the independent variable and which is the dependent variable.

- Point biserial correlation – used to correlate a continuous variable with a true dichotomous variable. It is equivalent to the Pearson's r correlation coefficient.
- Biserial correlation – used to correlate a continuous variable with a dichotomous variable which is based on an underlying continuous variable.
- One-way ANOVA – used when the categories on the independent variable are not related (for example, two or more separate groups), when variances of the groups are approximately equal and when a normal distribution is assumed. When any of the final two conditions cannot be met, the Kruskal-Wallis test can be used.
- Repeated measures ANOVA – used when the categories on the independent variable are related (for example, scores obtained at two or more points in time), when you can assume sphericity (equal variances between the differences in pairs of scores, although some statistical packages correct the estimates for this) and when a normal distribution is assumed. When the final condition cannot be met, the Friedman test can be used.
- Polyserial correlation coefficient – used to correlate a continuous variable with a variable measured at the ordinal level which is based on an underlying continuous variable.
- Pearson's r correlation coefficient – used to correlate two continuous variables when a normal distribution is assumed. When a normal distribution cannot be assumed, Spearman's rho correlation coefficient can be used.

5.2.2 How do I examine relationships/associations/ differences among more than two variables?

When you have more than two variables in your analysis, you need to work out whether you have additional independent variables, additional dependent variables or additions of both types of variables. You also need to consider how you intend to treat these variables. This latter decision should most often be guided by theoretical considerations and your research questions. We will look at each situation in turn.

5.2.2.1 I have several independent variables (or covariates) and one dependent variable

When the independent variables are categorical and the dependent variable is continuous, then you can choose from some extensions of the analysis of variance (ANOVA) model. If you have two independent variables, you can run a two-way ANOVA; if you have three independent variables, you can run a three-way ANOVA, and so on. Let's take the two-way ANOVA as an example. In a two-way ANOVA, if both independent variables represent independent groups, then this is known as a two-way between-groups ANOVA; if both independent variables represent related scores (for example, points in time), then this is known as a two-way repeated measures or a two-way within-subjects ANOVA; if one independent variable represents independent groups and the other represents related scores, then this is known as a two-way between-within or a two-way mixed ANOVA.

It may be that you have included extra variables in your analyses not because you are interested in the effect of the different levels of these variables on the dependent variable, but because you want to 'control for' the effects of these additional variables. In this situation, we would refer to these additional variables as covariates. An example of this is where you are conducting a study to evaluate an intervention which aims to reduce anxiety among participants. In the study, you have measured anxiety before the intervention was administered (pre-test) and then after the intervention was complete (post-test). You have two groups in the study, an intervention group and a control group. Your interest is in whether the anxiety levels of the intervention group are lower than the anxiety levels for the control group at the post-test stage. Of course, you need to take account of the anxiety levels at the pre-test stage, as it is the change in anxiety caused by the intervention which is the important thing. One way of dealing with this is to conduct a two-way mixed ANOVA, where the time points (pre-test and post-test) constitute a repeated measures independent variable and the groups (control and intervention) constitute the between-groups independent variable.

An alternative approach is to conduct an analysis of covariance (ANCOVA). In this case, the scores on the post-test are considered the dependent variable, the two groups (control and intervention) constitute a between-groups independent variable and the pre-test anxiety scores are treated as a covariate. The ANCOVA will provide a slightly different analysis than the two-way mixed ANOVA. In the two-way mixed ANOVA, we are asking whether there is a difference between the two groups in the change in anxiety scores. In the ANCOVA, we are asking whether there is a difference between the two groups in their post-test anxiety scores, after we take account of their pre-test anxiety scores. In summary, the two-way mixed ANOVA is concerned only with change but the ANCOVA is also concerned with how the starting point for individuals (the pre-test score) might impact on the amount of change. Therefore, the ANCOVA is often a more powerful analysis in this situation.

When you have covariates in your study design, another alternative is to conduct a regression analysis. Linear regression is similar to ANCOVA, although all variables are considered to be covariates in a regression. The distinction is more theoretical than statistical. Regression is used to build a model where several variables are considered to be important in explaining the variance in a dependent variable. For example, if you believe that anxiety scores could be explained by whether someone received an intervention, their anxiety at some time in the past, the level of social support available to them and the coping strategies they adopt, then you could measure all these variables and use regression to tell you to what extent each of the variables considered is related to anxiety (after controlling for all the other variables in the analysis).

Independent variables (as distinct from covariates, using the ANOVA terminology) are categorical variables; covariates are continuous or dichotomous variables, although other categorical variables can be used if they are converted into dummy variables (see Section 5.3). In all ANOVA or ANCOVA models or linear regression, normality is assumed, and the dependent variable is assumed to be continuous; but there are several types of regression which permit categorical dependent variables.

5.2.2.2 I have several dependent variables

With several dependent variables, this may simply mean that you need to conduct your chosen tests several times (one test for every dependent variable, as most statistical tests include only one dependent variable). However, there are some situations where you can potentially reduce the amount of analysis by combining your dependent variables into a single composite, which represents a linear combination of the dependent variables. It should be clear that there must be some conceptual basis for doing this. That is, the dependent variables should be conceptually related. If this is possible, then a multivariate analysis of variance (MANOVA) could be used. The MANOVA is simply an extension of any ANOVA to more than one dependent variable (for example, you can have a one-way MANOVA, a two-way MANOVA, a repeated measures MANOVA, a MANCOVA and so on). The resulting test indicates whether a difference exists between the groups, and if this is the case, then you might wish to examine each dependent variable separately to see where this difference lies.

As with all analysis of variance and regression (often grouped as the general linear model) approaches, specific assumptions apply to specific tests, so you should make yourself aware of these prior to undertaking the analyses.

5.3   Common problems

The brief guide provided in Section 5.2 will help to refresh your memory about statistical analyses and point you in the right direction when considering your choice of statistical tests. I have not provided a detailed discussion of these tests as such information is easily accessible from a number of books (for example, Greer & Mulhern, 2001; Brace et al., 2009). However, in my experience, even after consulting statistics textbooks, trainee psychologists can encounter statistical dilemmas which they have difficulty resolving. I think this might be because these issues speak to the more philosophical branch of statistics, and (unfortunately) the teaching of statistics in psychology seems to focus more on the 'rules' of statistics. Consequently, students of psychology believe that there are fixed, specific ways of conducting statistical analyses, and they are not prepared for the situations (which commonly arise in applied research) which require a judgement to be made about the most reasonable approach. Understandably, the uncertainty is troubling and confusing. Therefore, in this section, I have tried to provide some guidance to resolving some commonly encountered dilemmas. I would also recommend that you read the information presented in Section 9.2, in which I have tried to highlight some of the statistical issues that seem to occur to trainees at the write-up stage, but that should probably be considered earlier in the research process.

5.3.1   I have conducted several significance tests – do I need to adjust my significance level for multiple testing?

Usually, when you conduct a significance test, you use a cut-off value of 0.05. In other words, if your probability (or significance) value falls below 0.05, you conclude that you can reject your null hypothesis. This cut-off point is known as the alpha value (α). By choosing a value of 0.05 as the alpha value, we are accepting a 5 % chance of making a Type I error. A Type I error is where we decide to reject a null hypothesis which is, in reality, true. Convention suggests that you should not use an alpha value higher than 0.05. That is, you should not be prepared to accept a higher risk of a Type I error than 5 %.

If the risk of making a Type I error is 5 %, this means that (on average) 5 out of 100 (or 1 out of 20) significance tests that are conducted will result in a Type I error. The important principle here is that the more significance tests conducted, the greater the likelihood that a Type I error will be made. Therefore, if we want the Type I error rate for a group of significance tests to remain at no more than 5 % overall, we need to adjust the alpha value for each individual significance test. A common approach to making this adjustment is the Bonferroni method. The Bonferroni method is applied by dividing the alpha value for each significance test by the total number of significance tests conducted. For example, if you have a group of five significance tests, then you would divide alpha by five. Therefore, to ensure an overall Type I error rate of 5 % for the five significance tests conducted, the significance (or probability) value for each individual significance test would need to be less than 0.01 before you would reject the null hypothesis.

This principle of adjusting alpha within a group of significance tests is uncontroversial. However, there is more controversy about *when* this adjustment should be applied. In other words, there is some debate about what constitutes a 'group' of significance tests. Some researchers have argued that alpha values should be adjusted on the basis of the total number of significance tests conducted within a study; others argue that adjustments should be made only for the number of significance tests which focus on a single hypothesis (see Perneger, 1998). The following guidance might prove helpful for you in deciding how you should treat your data.

I recommend that you adjust alpha based on the number of significance tests conducted to address a single hypothesis. For example, your study might be designed to evaluate an intervention by comparing the results from an intervention and control group. This could be done using a single significance test. However, if the effectiveness of the intervention is measured by more than one outcome measure, then you might need more than one significance test, and you would need to adjust alpha for the number of tests conducted (depending on how related the outcome measures are, although distinct outcome measures will probably result from distinct and separate hypotheses). Additionally, if you wish to conduct subgroup analysis (that is, examining differences between subgroups of the intervention and control group), this will require further significance testing and adjustment of alpha.

If you are conducting a study of a more exploratory nature where there are no specific hypotheses to be tested, but a series of research questions, then there may be no requirement to make adjustments for the number of significance tests conducted. However, there is a requirement for you to interpret the significance tests while bearing in mind the effects of the Type I error. In this situation, I recommend that you report the exact p values (where possible) of all your significance tests and that you try to make sense of the pattern of results. In other words, if you have conducted 20 significance tests and only 1 test is statistically significant, it would not be appropriate to focus on the significant result and ignore the other 19 tests. In fact, it is more likely that this significant result has arisen by chance, and the overall pattern suggests no relationship between the variables.

5.3.2 What is the difference between clinical significance and statistical significance?

Finding a statistically significant result in your analysis is important. It gives you confidence in your findings, and it helps you infer your results to the population of interest. But the information provided by knowing that a result was statistically significant is limited. Usually, when a significance (or probability) value is less than 0.05, we conclude that we have a statistically significant finding. What this means is that there is a less than 5 % chance that we would have found a result of at least this size if the null hypothesis was true. Logically, then, our conclusion is that the null hypothesis probably is not true. But knowing that a result was statistically significant does not provide us with one essential piece of information which is required in order to make sense of our result – the effect size. It is not sufficient to focus on statistical significance in your analyses; you must also consider the effect size.

An introduction to the effect size is provided in Section 2.4. In summary, effect sizes provide an indication of the size of the difference/relationship found in your analysis. The effect size will help you to determine whether the effect found in your analysis is clinically significant. A clinically significant effect means an effect which is likely to be important in a clinical setting. It is useful to speak with clinicians at the design stage of your research to determine what the threshold for clinical significance on your outcome measures might be. In fact, this might be essential to allow you to calculate the required sample size for your study (see Box 3.1). In applied research, clinical and statistical significance are important, and both should be addressed in a research study. One does not assume the other. That is, it is possible to obtain a statistically significant effect which is not clinically significant, and it is possible to obtain a clinically significant effect which is not statistically significant. In the former case, you can be confident that you have found a difference/relationship, but this difference/relationship is small and not likely to have an important impact on the outcomes of interest. In the latter case, you have found an important difference/relationship in your sample, but you cannot be confident that this effect can be inferred from the sample to the population of interest.

5.3.3 I didn't manage to attain the required sample size – how can I conduct analysis on my small sample?

This is really a composite of two separate questions which I am often asked. The first question is about what to do when you do not attain the sample size suggested by the *a priori* sample size calculation. The good news is that this might not be a problem. Sample size calculations are a best estimate of the sample size that will be required for your study. Therefore, your sample size calculation might slightly overestimate the number you need in order to have sufficient power in your analysis. You will never know for sure until you have conducted your analysis. (However, if you are reading this in advance of collecting your data, remember that the sample size calculation can also underestimate the number required, so it is not a good idea to aim lower than the sample size calculation suggests).

The second question is about what to do when your sample size is small and your analysis does not have sufficient power. In these situations, you are unlikely to obtain any statistically significant findings, and the output from your analyses can be very disheartening. Of course, given more time, you could simply continue with your data collection until you attained the required sample size, but on a time-limited training programme, you do not have this luxury. Note that I am referring to situations here where the small sample size has arisen out of a situation which was beyond your control and could not have been foreseen at the planning stage. If this is not the case, then an assessor might conclude that this was a badly planned study and, consequently, does not demonstrate competence in research design.

When faced with a small sample, the reality is that you cannot make useful inferences to your population of interest and trying to do so will demonstrate a lack of awareness of the limitations of your research, so this should be openly acknowledged. However, this does not render the data useless. In this case, you need to steer the focus away from statistical significance and more towards clinical significance. You might still be able to make some interesting and useful conclusions about the effects demonstrated within your sample. In order to achieve this, an in-depth exploration of your data is required. There is a group of statistical techniques known as exploratory data analysis techniques which is useful to employ to help with this in-depth exploration (see Greer & Mulhern, 2001). I suggest that you rehearse the argument for using exploratory data analysis in preference to statistical inference before your viva exam (if you have one on your training programme). Also, see the section on bootstrapping in this chapter.

5.3.4   How should I deal with non-completers/missing values?

Missing values in your data will range from a participant omitting an item or two on a questionnaire to a participant not providing any data at a follow-up data collection point. In addition to comparing non-completers with completers to examine the effects of attrition, as discussed in Chapter 9, you will be faced with the dilemma about how to deal with these missing values.

In the case where a small proportion of items from a questionnaire have been omitted, many questionnaires have suggested procedures for dealing with this. For example, some scoring instructions for questionnaires indicate that if more than 50 % of the items on a scale are completed, then you can calculate the scale score based on the completed items, thereby resolving the problem.

When larger portions of data have been omitted or where the procedure outlined in the previous paragraph does not apply, then you can either treat the person's score on the measure(s) as missing, which means they will not be included in any analysis of these variables, or you can estimate their score and use this estimate in your analysis. Estimating scores will allow you to maximise your sample size and so increase the power of your analysis, but the basis for the estimation needs to be considered thoroughly, and no matter how rigorous this is it is still an estimated score, not a score obtained from a participant. Consequently, not everyone is comfortable with this procedure.

Most statistical software now includes procedures for replacing missing values, but you need to consider carefully the procedure that the software is using and whether it is appropriate for your purposes. One procedure for replacing missing values is based on regression analysis. Let's take an example where a longitudinal study involves collecting data on the same measure at four points in time, but some of our participants did not provide data at time four. In this case, we can use regression analysis to predict scores at time four from the scores at times one, two and three. That is, we have a regression model where score at time four is the outcome variable and scores at times one, two and three are independent variables. This will provide a regression equation (based on those participants who have completed all time points). We can then input the scores at times one, two and three for each individual in turn who omitted time four, and the equation will provide us with a predicted time four score.

When participants drop out of an intervention group, you should still try to collect data from them on the outcome measures at the times these measures are to be administered. It might be the case that the person no longer wishes to engage with the intervention, but they might still be willing to provide data for the study. There are two approaches to treating this data in your analysis. Intention to treat analysis means that participants remain in the groups they were allocated to for the purposes of analysis. In other words, even if someone drops out of an intervention group, their data will be included in the intervention group when it comes to the analysis. The principle here is that people drop out of interventions in real life, so if we want to get an estimate of the effectiveness of the intervention as it will be delivered in a real life setting, then we need to take account of these drop outs and the negative effect they might have on the overall effectiveness of the intervention. Alternatively, you can choose a per-protocol analysis. In this case, participants' data are included in the intervention group if they completed the intervention as per the study protocol. This type of analysis provides an indication of the efficacy of the intervention, that is, the effect that the intervention can have if everyone adheres to it. Often, in evaluations of interventions, researchers will provide both types of analysis, as they communicate different and complementary information.

If the decisions you make about how you treat your data still leave you with some missing values, then you need to decide whether to omit these participants from your analysis entirely. That is, whether you should restrict all your analyses to participants who have provided a full data set only, thereby including the same group of people in all analyses, or whether you should include anyone in the analysis that you can, which means that different people will enter and leave as different analyses are conducted. The decision will be based on how the different analyses that you are conducting are related to each other and the conclusions that you want to draw.

5.3.5 How do I test for mediation and/or moderation?

Moderation and mediation refer to specific forms of action that a third variable (let's call it variable M) has on the relationship between two variables (let's call these variables A and B). I have grouped moderation and mediation together as they are often confused with each other, but I will address each in turn.

Moderation occurs when the nature of the relationship between A and B is dependent on the level of variable M which is present. For example, a study finds that there is a moderate relationship between attitudes towards organ donation (variable A) and intention to sign the organ donor register (variable B). The study further finds that among those people who know of someone who is on the waiting list for an organ transplant, the relationship between attitudes to organ donation and intention to sign the organ donor register is very strong, whereas among those people who do not know of someone who is on the waiting list for an organ transplant, the relationship between attitudes to organ donation and intention to sign the organ donor register is weak to moderate. Therefore, it appears that whether you know of someone who is on the organ donor register moderates the relationship between attitudes to organ donation and intention to sign the organ donor register.

Moderation is usually assessed by examining interactions between the independent (or predictor) variable and the potential moderator. In the example above, this would mean examining the interaction between attitudes to organ donation and whether you know of someone who is on the organ donor register. To create an interaction term, we multiply one variable with the other, after centring both variables. Centring means subtracting the mean score from each score in the variable so that the mean score of the centred variable is zero. If you are using an ANOVA approach to your analysis, then most statistical software packages will create an interaction term for you (see Brace et al., 2009).

Mediation occurs when the relationship between A and B is explained by M. For example, the relationship between attitudes to organ donation and whether you sign the organ donor register might be mediated by your intention to sign the organ donor register. In their classic paper on the subject, Baron and Kenny (1986) outline four steps in establishing mediation:

1. There must be a relationship between A and B. There is some disagreement about whether this step is necessary, for example, when M acts as a suppressor variable (see MacKinnon, Fairchild & Fritz, 2007).
2. There must be a relationship between A and M.
3. There must be a relationship between M and B after controlling for A.
4. The relationship between A and B becomes zero after controlling for M. This demonstrates complete mediation. If the relationship between A and B reduces considerably after controlling for M, this demonstrates partial mediation.

Mediation is most easily demonstrated using hierarchical regression. Conduct a hierarchical regression where variable B is the dependent variable, variable A is entered into the first block as an independent variable and variable M is entered into the block 2. The resulting regression coefficients table for block 1 will provide a measure of the relationship between A and B (addressing step 1). The coefficients for block 2 will provide a measure of the relationship between M and B after controlling for A (step 3) and will provide a measure of the relationship between A and B after controlling for M. The difference between the standardised coefficient provided for this latter relationship and the standardised coefficient provided in block 1 will indicate whether the relationship between And B reduces considerably when M is controlled for (step 4). The final analysis is to ensure that there is a relationship between A and M (step 2), which can be assessed using a correlation coefficient.

With this information, we can also assess whether there is a statistically significant indirect effect of the independent variable (A) on the dependent variable (B) via the mediator (M). This is assessed using a Sobel test. The Sobel test is useful for large samples but a bootstrapping approach (see Section 5.3.12) to mediation can be used in all cases. Further information about the Sobel test and an interactive calculator, and information about the bootstrapping approach to mediation can be found in Preacher & Hayes (2004; 2008) and at: http://www.people.ku.edu/~preacher/sobel/sobel.htm.

In mediation, the assumption is that A causes M. In moderation, this assumption is not made. The decision about whether a third variable is a potential mediator or a potential moderator should be based largely on some theoretical assumption. It is one thing to argue that a variable is a mediator or a moderator on the basis of statistical evidence, but if the proposed relationship does not make sense conceptually, then it is only a statistical artefact. In other words, you should have a rationale for investigating mediation and/or moderation and so you should be able to specify this at the proposal stage of your research. Some more recent debate about the conceptualisation of mediators and moderators is provided in Kraemer, Kiernan, Essex & Kupfer (2008).

5.3.6 How do I decide the content of the blocks in hierarchical regression and the order of entry?

Hierarchical regression is a form of regression where the covariates are entered sequentially either individually or in groups, known as blocks. Hierarchical regression is used when we want to know how entering a block of variables to a regression model affects the parameters of the existing model. For example, imagine that the aim of your study is to attempt to explain why some men with heart disease experience high levels of symptoms of depression and others do not. You might collect information on the length of time the men have had heart disease, any other illnesses they have and the quality of social support available to them, as you believe all of these variables are relevant in explaining heart disease. In your analysis, you want to know to what extent the medical variables (time since diagnosis and number of other illnesses) explain symptoms of depression and then how much the social support variable adds to the explanation of depression. In this case, you would enter the medical variables in block 1 and the social support variable in block 2. The resulting R^2 value from block 1 in the regression output will tell you the amount of variance in depression that is explained by medical variables. The difference between the R^2 value from block 1 and the R^2 value from block 2 will tell you how much social support adds to the explanation of variance in depression, after we have accounted for the medical variables.

It should be clear from this description that the order of entry of the blocks will affect the conclusions you can draw from your analysis. Although the order of entry will not affect the regression coefficients or the R^2 value in the final model (when all blocks are entered), it will affect the change in the R^2 value. By entering a block earlier, it is being given a better chance at explaining a higher proportion of the variance in the outcome variable. Therefore, the order of entry and the content of your blocks should be guided by some theoretical rationale or by the specific need of the research question. You should be able to specify this at the proposal stage of your research.

5.3.7   How do I create dummy variables to use in a regression analysis, and how do I interpret them?

Regression analysis can accept dichotomous variables as covariates but not categorical variables with more than two categories. If you have a categorical variable with more than two categories that you wish to use in a regression analysis, then it needs to be converted into dummy variables. Dummy variables are dichotomous variables, and for any categorical variable, you need to create a number of dummy variables equal to the number of categories minus one. In other words, if you have a variable with four categories, you will need to create three dummy variables to represent it adequately. Dummy variables are created as follows:

- Choose one of the categories in your variable to be the reference category. This is the category against which all the other categories in your variable will be compared. Therefore, it needs to be meaningful. For example, choose a well-defined category, not a category which captures 'other' responses, and if your categories are ranked, choose a category at one extreme.
- Create a dummy variable with scores of 0 and 1 for every other category. For example, if your variable has four categories and you

choose category 1 as your reference category, then create a dummy variable for categories 2, 3 and 4. To create a dummy variable for category 2 (let's call it D2), give everyone in category 2 a score of 1 and give everyone else a score of 0. To create a dummy variable for category 3 (D3), give everyone in category 3 a score of 1 and give everyone else a score of 0. Do the same for category 4.

- This will give you three dummy variables. When you enter all three the dummy variables together in a regression analysis, they will be compared to the reference category. In other words, D2 will not represent category 2 versus all other categories but will actually represent category 2 versus category 1 (your reference category). D3 will represent category 3 versus category 1, and so on. It is the combination of scores on the variables that allows the regression analysis to perform this neat manoeuvre, so be warned that if you do not enter all dummy variables at the same time, then this process will not work.

To interpret a dummy variable, you must remember how the variable was coded (so it is worth making a note of this somewhere when you create the dummy variables). In the example above, D2 is the dummy variable which represents category 2 versus category 1 (in the context of a regression model). In this case, category 2 was given a score of 1 and category 1 had a score of 0. Therefore, a positive regression coefficient for D2 suggests that those in category 2 have a higher score on the outcome variable than those on category 1, and a negative regression coefficient suggests that those on category 1 have a higher score on the outcome variable than those on category 2.

5.3.8 Should I use stepwise regression or enter all my covariates into a regression model

Stepwise regression enters and/or removes variables from a regression model on the basis of specified statistical criteria. This is an alternative to the 'enter' method of regression, where all variables are forced into the model. Which approach is appropriate depends on the aim of your regression analysis. Where a regression analysis is being conducted to test a theoretical model, then the content of the model should be driven by the theory. In this case, the regression analysis is a method of establishing the extent to which the theoretical model is supported by the data. Therefore, the 'enter' method is appropriate. If a stepwise analysis is used, then the content of the model would be driven by the sample data, which is not appropriate. Of course, testing a theoretical model requires you to have a sufficient sample size to ensure adequate power in your analysis.

Alternatively, a regression analysis can be conducted for the purposes of building a model. In this, more exploratory, type of research you will not have a theory that clearly guides the variables that should be included in the analysis. Instead, you have probably collected data on a number of variables which you believe (with some justification) are likely to be related to the outcome measure (dependent variable) of interest. In this situation, regression analysis is used to determine the best fitting model. In other words, regression analysis is used to indicate which variables (among the variables included in the model) are most strongly related to the outcome measure. A straightforward approach to meeting this aim is to use the 'enter' method. When all variables are entered into the model, you can see the nature of the (partial) relationship between each variable and the outcome measure. However, in some cases this might be an unsatisfactory solution, especially if there are many variables in the model which have a weak and non-significant relationship with the outcome measure. In this case, the important variables might be hidden in a large table and the overall fit of the model is likely to be low. To resolve this issue, you might wish to refine your model to eliminate the variables that are making little contribution to the model and thereby highlight the important variables and improve the model fit. This can be achieved through some form of stepwise regression.

There are different types of stepwise regression, and you should consult a statistics advisor to discuss the most appropriate method for your data. Whichever method you choose, you need to be aware of the implications of using stepwise regression for your conclusions about your analysis. Firstly, stepwise regression will probably provide you with the most parsimonious model on the basis of your data. This does not mean that the variables that were excluded were unimportant, but only that the variables that were included in the final model were considered more important in terms of their partial relationship with the outcome variable. Secondly, some stepwise procedures use statistical significance to include/exclude variables in the final model. If this is the case in your analysis, then the content of the final model will greatly depend on your sample size. That is, the larger your sample size, the more likely it is that a larger number of variables will be included in the final model. Finally, if you exclude variables from the model on the basis of low correlations between the variable and the outcome measure, then you are running the risk of missing useful suppressor variables.

Suppressor variables are variables that have a low correlation with the outcome variable but which might explain a significant amount of variance in other covariates in your regression model. As a result, their inclusion in your regression model is useful because they help to explain some of the error variance in the covariates. In summary, then, stepwise regression is useful in some situations, but you must be careful about its interpretation.

5.3.9 How robust are statistical tests to violations of their assumptions?

Parametric statistical tests make assumptions about the distribution on which the test is based. The often discussed assumptions made by parametric tests are an assumption of normality and an assumption of homogeneity of variance. Often psychology graduates leave their under-graduate programme with the notion that you don't need to worry too much about these assumptions as the tests are fairly robust to any violation of their assumptions. I think this is a dangerous premise to work with, as the parameters of 'fairly robust' are not clear. In other words, it is not always clear when a violation of the assumptions underlying these tests is problematic.

Huck (2009, p. 207) provides evidence that t-tests are robust to violations of the assumptions of normality and/or equal variances when the sample sizes in the two groups are equal and the sample size in each group is 25 or greater. Sample sizes smaller than this are problematic in that the t-test has an elevated Type I error rate. This fits with the notion of the Central Limit Theorem, which tells us that the sampling distribution will be normal regardless of whether the population distribution is normal as long as your sample size is large. Large is defined as a sample size of approximately 30 or more, in this context. However, when sample sizes are smaller than this and/or when group sizes are unequal, then the assumptions underlying the statistical test need to be checked.

Some statistical tests do not assume normality of the sampling distribution, but assume normality of the errors or residual scores. This is the case in tests that belong to the general linear model family, such as ANOVAs and linear regression. In this situation, the assumptions need to be checked regardless of the sample size, as violation of the assumptions can affect the fit indices of the model.

5.3.10 How do I test for the assumption of normality of residual scores?

A residual is the difference between an actual value and the predicted value (often a mean score) for the group/category from which that value was taken. For example, if we have a data set containing scores on a test for males and females, then the residual would be the difference between a person's score on the test and the mean score for males if the person was male, or between the person's score on the test and the mean score for females if the person was female. For example:

Table 5.3 Calculating residual scores

Score	Gender	Mean score	Residual
10	Male		10–10 = 0
11	Male		11-10 = 1
11	Male	50/5 = 10	11-10 = 1
10	Male		10–10 = 0
8	Male		8-10 = -2
10	Female		10–12 = -2
9	Female		9-12 = -3
13	Female	60/5 = 12	13-12 = 1
14	Female		14-12 = 2
14	Female		14-12 = 2

The residual tells us the amount of error in our model in terms of the fitted values. Remember that we are using the group mean as a value that represents all values in that group. Therefore, the residual informs us how well the mean represents each value in the group.

In more complex analyses (that is, analyses with several variables such as in an ANOVA or multiple linear regression), the calculation of a residual score by hand is not as straightforward. Helpfully, most statistical software packages will calculate residuals for you. The simplest, and most effective, method of checking the assumption of normality is to plot these residual scores on a graph, such as a histogram. By examining the graph, you can decide whether the distribution is approximately normal and is free from outliers. Remember that the distribution need only approximate normality, so your visual judgement is usually sufficient.

In situations where you have a small number of values in your distribution, it might be difficult to make sense of the graph, and, in this case, a statistic might be useful. One commonly used statistic is the Kolmogorov-Smirnov test. This test will examine your distribution and compare it against a normal distribution. If the test returns a statistically significant result, it suggests that your distribution of scores differs significantly from the normal distribution. I caution against using these tests with large sample sizes, as they are likely to indicate that even small and irrelevant departures from normality are significant.

5.3.11   How do I test for the assumption of sphericity?

When you conduct an ANOVA with a repeated measures factor, you need to examine the assumption of sphericity. Basically, sphericity refers to the equality of the variances of the differences among levels of the repeated measures factor. In other words, we calculate the differences between each pair of levels of the repeated measures factor and then calculate the variance of these difference scores. Sphericity requires that the variances for each set of difference scores are equal.

Fortunately, when you conduct an ANOVA with a repeated measures factor on SPSS you will automatically obtain a test for sphericity, known as Mauchly's test. Interpreting this test is straightforward: when the significance level of the Mauchly's test is less than 0.05, we cannot assume sphericity; when the significance level is greater than 0.05 we can assume sphericity.

Fortunately, again, when you conduct an ANOVA with a repeated measures factor SPSS will automatically generate corrections for violations of sphericity, for example, the Greenhouse-Geisser and the Huynh-Feldt corrections. To correct for sphericity, these corrections alter the degrees of freedom, thereby altering the significance value of the F ratio. Another option when sphericity is violated is to use the multivariate test (which again is provided automatically by SPSS when you ask for an ANOVA with a repeated measures factor). However, multivariate tests can be less powerful than their univariate counterparts. In general, the following guideline is useful: when you have a large violation of sphericity (epsilon < 0.7) and your sample size is greater than (10 + number of levels of the repeated measures factor), then multivariate tests are more powerful; in other cases, the univariate test should be preferred. The epsilon value can be found on the Mauchly's test output.

5.3.12   What is bootstrapping?

When assumptions, such as normality, are violated, one option is to transform your data so that they meet the assumptions of the test you wish to use. However, transforming your data does not always result in the desired outcome and can create variables which are difficult to interpret. This often happens when your data are inherently skewed (that is, it is not reasonable to assume that your data are normally distributed in the population) or when your sample size is small. In this situation, a potential solution might be bootstrapping.

Bootstrapping avoids the need for us to make assumptions about the sampling distribution. Rather, the properties of the sampling distribution are estimated from the sample data. In other words, we create a sampling distribution which is specific to our data. Recall that a sampling distribution is a distribution of a sample statistic (such as the mean) created from an infinite number of samples (of a specified fixed size) drawn from the population. That is, we take a sample from the population, calculate the mean score for the sample and plot the mean score on a graph. We then take a second sample from the population, calculate the mean score for this sample and plot on the graph. We repeat this procedure an infinite number of times, and the resulting distribution of mean scores is known as our sampling distribution (of the mean). Obviously, this is a hypothetical distribution, hence the requirement to make assumptions about it rather than direct observations.

In bootstrapping, we mirror the procedure of creating a sampling distribution, but this time we do this in reality, not hypothetically. In this case, our sample data are treated like the population distribution. We take a smaller sample (a sub-sample) from our sample data and calculate the statistic of interest (for example, the mean score). We then replace the data and take a second sub-sample and calculate the statistic of interest. This is often referred to as re-sampling. We repeat this procedure a large number of times (the more times, the better, but 2000 samples is often recommended as a minimum), and the result is a bootstrap sampling distribution. As with our theoretical sampling distribution, the standard deviation of the bootstrap sampling distribution represents the standard error, which is the basis for significance tests. There is no clear information about the size of sample required for bootstrapping to work, although some authors have shown that this procedure works with sample sizes as small as 20 (Yung & Chan, 1999).

Bootstrapping has only relatively recently become a feasible approach to conducting statistical analysis, with the advent of more powerful computers. However, many statistical software packages used by psychology trainees do not currently (by default) have a bootstrapping procedure which can be used to calculate different statistics of interest. In some cases, the bootstrapping procedures can be purchased as an add-on to your existing software.

5.4 Calculating sample size

Chapter 3 included a discussion on the importance of sample size calculations in quantitative research and provided an introduction to the principles of calculating sample size for your research proposal. This section aims to apply those principles to sample size calculations based on different analyses.

As mentioned in Chapter 3, the sample size calculation is based on your planned statistical analysis, the desired level of statistical power, the alpha value and the effect size. The alpha value is conventionally 0.05, and the minimum level of desired power is conventionally 0.8. The effect size is something that you must research. A statistics advisor will not be able to help you generate an effect size although they might be willing to help with the calculation of an effect size if you have provided the relevant data. The effect size should be calculated for your proposed primary analysis (for example, the analysis based on your primary outcome measure), and it is this proposed analysis which will guide the method of calculating the sample size. There are many freely available sample size calculators on the internet (for example, G-Power: http://www.psycho. uni-duesseldorf.de/abteilungen/aap/gpower3/), and this section does not intend to explore the mathematics underlying these calculations. Instead, the aim here is to provide a guide to the type of information that you need to obtain to enable the calculation of an effect size to input into a sample size calculation.

It is important to note at this point that sample size calculations are based on the final numbers that you want to have available for analysis, so any potential dropout rate must be factored in to your initial recruitment.

5.4.1   How do I calculate sample size for correlation or regression analysis?

Sample size calculation for analysis using a bivariate correlation coefficient is relatively straightforward and can readily be done by hand (see Box 5.3).

Box 5.1   Calculating sample size for a bivariate correlation coefficient

Sample size required to attain 80 % power, with alpha = 0.05, using a one-tailed test:

$$n = 1 + (2.5 / \rho)^2$$

where ρ = the expected correlation coefficient.

Sample size required to attain 80 % power, with alpha = 0.05, using a two-tailed test:

$$n = 1 + (2.8 / \rho)^2$$

where ρ = the expected correlation coefficient.

When you are planning a simple regression, the effect size of interest is the overall R^2 value for the regression model. In other words, you want to know the sample size required to detect the expected R^2 value (with a specified power and alpha), given the number of covariates in the model. So before conducting the sample size calculation, you will need to specify the required power (minimum = 0.8), alpha (usually 0.05), the number of covariates (which should be clear from your research proposal) and the R^2 value that you expect to find in your regression model. Calculating the sample size amounts to giving this information as input to a sample size calculator, such as GPower, but the difficulty often encountered is deciding on the R^2 value that you expect to find in your regression model. The simplest way to make this decision would be to base it on previous research. Yet often the model that you want to examine in your regression analysis has not been examined before (which is why you have chosen this as an area worthy of investigation), so no previous research exists which will provide you with an R^2 value for the proposed model. One solution to this problem is to conduct a pilot study to identify a suitable R^2 value, but usually time within a training programme does not permit this. Therefore, the R^2 value that you choose for your sample size calculation will often be one which is based on an amalgamation of different pieces of information. This information will be, for example:

- Previous research which presents a regression model comprised of some of the variables in your planned analysis (for example, a model that your proposed research aims to extend).
- Previous research which provides correlation coefficients between your covariates and your outcome variable.
- The judgement of experienced researchers in the area about the size of the relationships between the variables in your proposed analysis.

In summary, you are attempting to gather as much information as possible to allow you to make an informed judgement about the likely size of the R^2 value for your analysis.

When planning to conduct a hierarchical regression, you will need the same information that was required to calculate sample size for simple regression, but this time the effect size of interest is the change in R^2 value between one block and another.

5.4.2   How do I calculate sample size for t-tests or ANOVAS?

Calculating sample size for independent t-tests and paired t-tests, like correlation coefficients, can be done by hand (see Box 5.2).

When calculating sample size for ANOVA models, the effect size of interest is eta-squared (η^2). Eta-squared can be derived from an ANOVA table by dividing the sum of squares for the effect of interest by the total sum of squares (although most statistical software packages will perform this calculation for you). Similar to the R^2 value in a regression model, η^2 estimates the proportion of variance in the dependent variable that is explained by the independent variable(s). However, the value of η^2 is likely to decrease as more variables are added to the model, because the total sum of squares will increase. Therefore, a more useful effect size is partial η^2 which is the sum of squares for the effect of interest divided by (the sum of squares of the effect of interest + the error sum of squares). In a one-way ANOVA, partial η^2 and η^2 are equal. Small, medium and large effects are usually considered to be represented by η^2 values of 0.01, 0.06 and 0.14 respectively.

Box 5.2 Calculating sample size for t-tests

For independent t-tests

Sample size required per group to attain 80 % power, with alpha = 0.05, using a one-tailed test:

$$2*(2.5 / ES)^2$$

where ES = the expected effect size expressed as Cohen's d.
    Sample size required per group to attain 80 % power, with alpha = 0.05, using a two-tailed test:

$$2*(2.8 / ES)^2$$

where ES = the expected effect size expressed as Cohen's d.

For paired t-tests

Sample size required to attain 80 % power, with alpha = 0.05, using a one-tailed test:

$$(2.8 / ES)^2$$

where ES = the expected effect size expressed as Cohen's d.
    Sample size required to attain 80 % power, with alpha = 0.05, using a two-tailed test:

$$(2.8 / ES)^2$$

where ES = the expected effect size expressed as Cohen's d.

For a one-way between-groups ANOVA, you will want to know the sample size required to detect the expected η^2 value (with a specified power and alpha), given the number of groups in the analysis. So before conducting the sample size calculation, you will need to specify the required power (minimum = 0.8), alpha (usually 0.05), the number of groups (which should be clear from your research proposal) and the η^2 value that you expect to find in your ANOVA. Again, the main difficulty often encountered is deciding on the η^2 value that you expect to find in your ANOVA and a similar strategy applies as that suggested for the sample size calculation for regression. Additionally, the η^2 value can be estimated based on the minimum clinically important difference (see Box 3.1). A common problem encountered here is that η^2 values are often not reported in the research literature. In this case, look for the F ratio and the df values. These can be converted into partial η^2 values, using the following formula: $(df_{effect} * F) / [(df_{effect} * F) + df_{error}]$.

For a two-way (or more than two-way) between-groups ANOVA, the same information is required, and the sample size calculations for the main effects proceed in the same way as that outlined for the one-way ANOVA. The difference is that often the focus of interest is on the interaction, and you want to make sure that you have a sufficient sample size to attain the desired level of power for the analysis of this interaction. Therefore, an estimate of the effect size (partial η^2) for the interaction is required.

For repeated measures ANOVAs, the same information is required, and, in addition, you need to estimate the correlation among the repeated measures. Given that sphericity is an assumption of the repeated measures ANOVA, the correlation between any two levels of the repeated measures factors should be similar to the correlation between any other two levels of the repeated measures factor. When this is not the case, some sample size calculators will allow you to enter a correction for non-sphericity. However, it will be difficult to estimate this in advance of collecting your data, and, therefore, a MANOVA approach might be more appropriate. A MANOVA does not assume sphericity, but it will require a larger sample size to attain the same level of power as a repeated measures ANOVA, as the denominator df for the F ratio is based on the sample size rather than the sample size multiplied by the number of levels of the repeated measures factor (because the MANOVA creates a single linear combination from all the repeated measures levels).

5.4.3 How do I calculate sample size for chi-square?

For a chi-square analysis based on a contingency table, the effect size of interest is based on the difference between the observed and expected frequencies within each cell of the table. This effect size is commonly referred to as w. It is found using the following equation:

$$w = \sqrt{\sum \frac{(p_0 - p_1)^2}{p_0}}$$

where p_0 = the proportion of total cases expected in each cell if the 2 variables were independent (expected frequencies);

p_1 = the proportion of cases expected in each cell (observed frequencies).

6

Qualitative Research: General Questions

● ●

This chapter is intended to provide an indication of the key criteria for a good qualitative research project. It is recommended that the information presented here is read in conjunction with Chapter 3.

It is difficult, and would be naive, to attempt to convey everything that is important about qualitative research (or any other type of research) in a single book chapter. Indeed, there are many books which devote considerably more space to a discussion of qualitative research (for example, Murray & Chamberlain, 1999; Smith, 2008; Harper & Thompson, 2011), and this chapter is not meant to replace those books. Rather, this chapter intends to address the most commonly asked questions and problems that trainee health and clinical psychologists experience when undertaking a qualitative project.

One of the difficulties with condensing everything that is important about conducting qualitative research into a single chapter is that qualitative research is not a single entity. In general, it is true that quantitative research stems from a single epistemological and theoretical orientation, although the methods within quantitative research might differ. However, qualitative research is an umbrella term used for a range of methodologies based on a range of theoretical orientations. As such, there are many researchers who will object to any attempt to group these different approaches under the one label. They will argue that this is reductionist. But, to some extent, the purpose of this book is to be reductionist. The book aims to address trainees' concerns when designing and conducting different types of research, not to provide a comprehensive guide to conducting different types of research.

6.1 Study quality

In this section, I aim to provide a guide to the important points to consider to enhance the quality of a qualitative research project. The information presented in this section is not meant to be a rigid set of rules. This would be inappropriate for a number of reasons (two of them follow): firstly, no single set of rules would do justice to the range of approaches which might be included under the umbrella term of qualitative research; and secondly, prescribing methods of conducting qualitative research suggests that there are fixed and immovable ways in which qualitative research should be conducted. This would limit the flexibility which is a major benefit of the qualitative approach. Indeed, good qualitative research is often research which uses novel and innovative methods. This is not to say that you can do anything you like and call it qualitative research as this would suggest that qualitative research has no rigour. Rather what I am saying is that as long as your novel method is one which follows a clear set of principles and is consistent with your stated theoretical approach, there is no reason you should be constrained by the methods developed by others. However, in my experience, trainee psychologists are not comfortable with this message – they seem to consider it a little too vague to be helpful in guiding their specific project design. Consequently, some general guiding principles might be useful.

Many guidelines for conducting qualitative research already exist and the information that I present here has been influenced by some of these authors, notably Burns (1989), Elliott, Fischer & Rennie (1999), Yardley (2000) and Meyrick (2006).

6.1.1 *What type of sampling should I use?*

As with any type of research, the important thing about your choice of sampling strategy for qualitative research is that it has a clear rationale. Sampling for qualitative research is purposive. That is, the members of the sample are purposively chosen to add to the analysis in some meaningful way. In some cases, this might mean selecting a homogeneous group of participants who will be able to shed light on a particular issue. In other cases, it might mean selecting participants to meet the requirements of the development of theory and on the basis of the analysis conducted on the participants included up to that point (theoretical sampling).

Furthermore, the sample size required should also be based on the aim of the project. For example, where the development of a theory grounded in the data is the aim, data collection should stop when theoretical saturation has been reached. That is, when no new information is obtained from subsequent participants (when additional data confirms the information that has already been obtained). An a priori rule might be established to guide this. For example, you might indicate in your proposal that data collection will cease after no new information has been obtained from three consecutive participants. On the other hand, the aim of your research might be to convey a deep understanding of the experiences of someone living in a particular situation or with a particular condition in order to help us make sense of their experience. In this case, an argument could be made for conducting a single case analysis. In a sense, all qualitative research aims for data saturation, but it is the definition of this saturation which is important, for example, we can talk about theoretical saturation across a group of people or about saturation of information about a specified topic within an individual.

6.1.2 Do I need to specify the content of the interview schedule/guide?

There is an argument made by trainees sometimes that an interview schedule or guide is not appropriate at the proposal stage of their research as they want to explore the topic of interest with participants in a more open and flexible manner. Although the rationale for this argument is understandable, it is worth considering the following.

Firstly, it is unlikely that ethics committees will be prepared to approve a project without being provided with some indication and examples of the types of questions that you intend to ask in your data collection process. Secondly, having an interview guide does not mean that you are obliged not to deviate from this guide. It would be inappropriate to follow an interview guide in content and structure regardless of the responses provided by the participant. This is the anti-thesis of qualitative research. Thirdly, as a trainee psychologist, it is important that your supervisor is aware of the types of questions you intend to ask your participant(s) in order to ensure that the questions are relevant to the overall aim of the research, that they are presented in a way consistent with the approach of the research and that their scope is feasible within the time constraints. Finally, interview guides are, at the very least, good safety nets. In the case where you are speaking with a participant who is not very talkative and needs some prompting to steer him/her in the direction of the research aim or to elicit further information, it might be difficult to think of appropriate prompts (that is prompts which will steer the participants but not lead them) during the interview process. Spending some time doing this in advance and writing them down for consideration and feedback by other members of the research team is useful.

In summary, some kind of data collection guide is usually included in the qualitative research proposals submitted by health/clinical psychology trainees. The level of detail required will depend on the aim of your research and the method chosen, but in all cases the content of the guide should be justified in your proposal.

6.1.3   Should my proposal be informed by previous literature/my previous experience?

Another common misconception about qualitative research sometimes held by trainees is that it is research conducted in a theoretical vacuum. In other words, the research should not be contaminated by previous experiences or previous literature but the researcher should 'bracket' their previous knowledge to prevent introducing bias to the research. It is impossible to completely remove bias from research (qualitative or quantitative), and in qualitative research there is openness about this. Instead of pretending to be free from bias, the qualitative tradition suggests that you should make your bias clear to the reader to enable the reader to judge how this might have influenced the research process.

In qualitative research, participants are not treated as objects from which information is obtained. Rather it is recognised that the data which emanates is based on the interaction between the participant and the researcher – it is a product of the dyad and the process that takes place. Therefore, to fully understand where the data has been obtained, it is important not only to describe the participant(s) and their situation and the context and process of the data collection, but also to describe the theoretical perspective, situation and characteristics of the data collector in so far as they are relevant to the data collection process.

The misperception held by trainees probably derives from a misunderstanding of the concept of bracketing. In the qualitative literature, bracketing refers to attempts by the researcher to prevent their personal bias and assumptions influencing their collection and interpretation of the data. It does not mean pretending not to have these assumptions or avoiding reading literature in the area which might 'put ideas in your head'. It means being aware of these assumptions, attempting to prevent them interfering with the research process and reflecting on the extent to which they have.

In summary, all good research (qualitative or quantitative) will build on and be informed by previous literature in the area (where it exists). That is not to say that all good research should be theoretically driven.

It is the way in which this literature influences decisions that are made during the research process and the extent to which this influence is made clear which is important.

6.1.4   How do I analyse qualitative data?

The analysis of qualitative data is tied to the study design. Data analysis should be informed by the theoretical approach in the same way as the data collection, thereby ensuring a consistent approach to addressing the aim of the study. Therefore, to some extent, the data analysis procedure will be determined by the specific method chosen. Nevertheless, there are some general principles that apply.

The data analysis procedure should be transparent, and, in particular, the process by which the data was reduced to themes/categories and conclusions should be made explicit. There should be examples of data that led to certain conclusions and examples that help to illustrate the analytic process, to evidence that conclusions are grounded in the data. During the analysis process it is important to continue the process of reflection on how the conclusions are influenced by personal assumptions and biases, with a view to ensuring, among other things, that premature analytical closure is avoided. This occurs when you notice patterns in the data at an early stage in the analysis process and then interpret subsequent data in a way that fits with these early interpretations. Another potential cause of drawing conclusions without allowing the entire data set an equal chance of 'speaking' to you is where you place an emphasis on the most articulate or verbose participants. Although it is true that some participants will facilitate your conclusions more than others, it is important that your conclusions represent the breadth of responses provided by participants, including any counter examples. Remember that the point of qualitative research is not to summarise individuals' responses into an average but to represent the diversity and complexity of responses in a digestible format.

Your reflections on this element of the research process (the analysis phase) are crucial. The interpretation of qualitative data is a continuous process. You will think about potential patterns in the data and what this means not only when you are looking at the data but also when you are engaged in other activities (as a good qualitative study results from the immersion of the researcher in the data and the research process). It is important to be mindful of this and to try to articulate the processes that occur which result in your conclusions. Some trainees whom I have supervised have found it useful to timetable supervisory sessions devoted to this purpose in their research proposal.

6.1.4.1 Thematic analysis

At this point, I think it is worth including some discussion of the technique of thematic analysis. Thematic analysis is considered by some to represent a specific methodology, to be placed alongside those methodologies discussed in Chapter 7 (for example, see Braun & Clarke, 2006). However, I regard thematic analysis as a technique employed in the analysis of qualitative data which can be used within a range of methodological approaches. For example, thematic analysis can be used in the analysis of data within an interpretative phenomenological analysis methodology or in the analysis of data within a grounded theory methodology. Yet this does not mean that thematic analysis must always be used in the context of another specific methodology. For example, it is reasonable to follow a more generic phenomenological approach to gathering and making sense of data and to use a thematic analysis to help organise this data (see McCorry, Dempster, Clarke & Doyle, 2009 for an example of this approach). Consequently, thematic analyses can vary considerably, and so I think it is insufficient to state that you are analysing your data using thematic analysis. More information needs to be provided to help the reader understand what you hope to achieve from your thematic analysis and what type of approach you are taking to your thematic analysis.

Given that some type of thematic analysis provides the basis for a considerable amount of qualitative research, a good understanding of the process of thematic analysis is important and is a useful starting point in the training of qualitative researchers.

In basic terms, thematic analysis requires you to familiarise yourself with the data (usually a transcript of an interview or focus group); code the text (for example, indicating important information in the text by highlighting it and using words or phrases to summarise the information highlighted); and attempt to group the codes into themes. The outcome of a thematic analysis should be the identification of a small number of themes which adequately summarise the pertinent issues arising from the qualitative data, and these themes should be evidenced by the data. Although the process presented appears linear, a good thematic analysis will not be. Rather you will need to regularly revisit your codes and themes in the light of new data, and you need to be open to modifying your codes and themes to avoid premature closure. As mentioned earlier, reflecting on the analytic process is an essential part of any qualitative approach.

Box 6.1 provides an excerpt from an interview transcript. This transcript represents part of a much longer interview (selected from several interviews) that was conducted by a trainee clinical psychologist (Joanne Gallagher). Joanne's research aimed to explore the experiences of mothers of adolescent females who had self-harmed. The excerpt aims to demonstrate how text from a transcript is converted into codes. These codes were then integrated with codes from other parts of the transcript and from other transcripts and contributed to the generation of the three main (super-ordinate) themes identified in the research:

1. Challenging identity – view of self as parent; view of relationship with daughter
2. Feeling frustrated, helpless and powerless
3. Coping

Box 6.1   Extracting themes from an interview transcript

Initial annotations	Excerpt from interview transcript
Limbo- isolation	I'm left in limbo, I'm left at…not wanting to invade her privacy but knowing that the only way I am going to find out is by snooping. I'd really rather not, but she has a thing now that she's 'putting more burden on her parents'. She actually doesn't tell her dad stuff and she sort of feels 'mummy's enough on her plate' and for that I am angry. The only good thing I've felt from it, is that they often say 'that kids who self harm don't commit suicide'. Obviously something wasn't right. I would just be afraid. I would find, that at times she just closes off in her room and you can't reach her. I can't reach her, I don't know what's going on in her head. You don't know how much of it, is teenager's moodiness and with the bother of a separated family. You can't always bring things back to it being a broken home or…I don't know, sort of 'what's what' and I'm just going through a minefield a lot of the time.
Guilt- I'd really rather not – anger	
Trying to focus on positives	
Fear, helplessness	
Confused, lost	

Box 6.1 Continued

Hyper-vigilance	And I do sort of look. You know, I had no idea the first time round, it was her stomach and the second, it was her arms, but you know teenagers...they can pull on a hoodie, even just put them on around the house and you don't see. Now I look, if I see scissors or anything around her room and I'd say, "What are these doing here? You know I'd rather not find scissors in your room because I'm afraid" and she keeps razor blades in the bathroom and you know things like that. She's still very very unhappy and she's still very deep. And I certainly wouldn't rule out the fact that she wouldn't do it again. I don't know.
Trying to communicate concerns	
Uncertainty	

The initial annotations led to construction of the following codes:
Emotional reaction – fear and isolation; Coping response – attempting to control situation and emotional response to situation; Expression of anger – response to guilt?
Challenging view of daughter and parenting; Searching for understanding and explanations; Anxiety, fear for future; Trying to gain a sense of control, hyperviligance.

Source: Excerpt taken from Gallagher (2008).

Obviously, I would need to provide you with all the transcripts to allow you to see how this thematic analysis moved from initial codes to overarching themes. But, the transcripts run to many pages, so that is not practicable within the context of this book. However, I hope that the example in Box 6.1 provides you with some sense of how text is converted to codes.

The point in the research process at which a thematic analysis is conducted, how this analysis is integrated with other analyses in the research, the effect that this analysis has on the remainder of the research process and how the analysis contributes to the study findings will be determined by the theoretical approach and/or methodology that you have adopted for your research (see Chapter 7).

6.1.5 *If data needs to be transcribed, do I need to do it?*

Data transcription takes a considerable amount of time, especially if you are not trained in speed typing. As a result, trainees will often ask whether this is something they should spend their time on or whether a 'professional transcriber' could be paid to undertake this task. Before making the decision to let someone else transcribe the data, consider the following. Firstly, some qualitative approaches are based on an ongoing analysis and developing understanding of the data (rather than collecting all the data and then doing the analysis). Any transcriptions will, therefore, be conducted in small chunks, and the outsourcing of data transcription might prove to be a false economy. As it is important to understand the data as the process continues, you would need to pass your data recording to a transcriber, wait for them to transcribe the data and then spend time becoming familiar with the data and making sense of it. If you are transcribing the data, this will help in the process of becoming familiar with the data and will require you to revisit your recordings of the data. This will be time well spent.

Secondly, there are nuances in the recording of the data that only you will be alert to, for example, some non-verbal behaviour that was displayed by a participant to emphasise a particular point or some silent event in the environment of the interview that changed the course of conversation. These points might be lost if someone else transcribes the data but could prove to be important in helping you make sense of the data.

Thirdly, there is the issue of confidentiality. Recordings of qualitative interviews regularly include personal, sensitive discussion, and, in order to facilitate and encourage openness in the discussion, you will promise the participant confidentiality. If you intend to allow someone else (a transcriber) to hear the information, then at least you should have told the participant that this would be the case before they agreed to participate in the research, and obtained their consent for this.

6.1.6 *How do I know that my interpretations/conclusions about the data are correct?*

This is probably one of the most common concerns expressed by trainees who are relatively new to the world of qualitative research. Trainees are anxious to know that their interpretations of the data are the right ones and that their assessor will not have a different interpretation that will cast doubt on the research competence of the trainee. I think this is a direct result of the undergraduate training of psychology students which, to a large extent, is embedded in a positivist epistemology. As a consequence, trainees are concerned with identifying the single, correct solution – the single truth that is out there, waiting to be found, staring everyone else (including their assessor) in the face but which they might fail to discover. This anxiety can be alleviated only by an acceptance that qualitative research does not operate with this philosophy; that what you will be presenting is your interpretation of the data and that this might legitimately differ from others. The important thing is that your interpretation is logical, based in the data, transparent, coherent, credible and not presented as the correct solution but as your solution which is influenced by your assumptions.

In order to alleviate this anxiety, trainees will often build checking procedures into their research proposal. As it happens, these procedures can be valuable, but often not, for the reason intended by the trainee. That is, these procedures are useful methods of checking the credibility of your conclusions, not of checking whether your conclusions are correct. These procedures are sometimes referred to as triangulation, which refers to examining the extent to which different perspectives on the issue coincide. These different perspectives could be the perspectives of different analysts, the inclusion of the participants' perspectives or the comparison of conclusions with external data. Given the broad meaning of the term 'triangulation' as it is currently used, I prefer to avoid it and to be more specific about the type of credibility check being discussed.

Two common credibility checks employed are the engagement of multiple analysts and respondent verification. Multiple analysts are used in different ways. In some cases, there is a main analyst and an auditor, who checks the process of converting data into conclusions to ensure that the conclusions are supported by the data. In other situations, more than one analyst might independently conduct an analysis of the data and draw conclusions. Another approach is for a second analyst to conduct an analysis of a selection of the data to ensure that the process of converting data to conclusions was adhered to. Whatever the method chosen, the aim of the process should not be to achieve the same outcomes. That is, this is not a method of checking inter-rater reliability. The aim of this process is to identify alternative credible explanations for the patterns detected in the data and to create discussion among the research team about the reasons for these discrepancies in interpretations and how these discrepancies further the understanding of the data. An additional aim is to ensure that the data coding process was applied in the manner described in the write-up of the paper.

Respondent verification refers to the process where the participants in the study are presented with the research team's interpretations and are asked to consider whether these conclusions resonate with their experience. It might appear that there is a strong rationale for including this type of credibility check, because the qualitative report is meant to reflect the experiences of the participants. Yet this depends on your theoretical position. Some might argue that the qualitative report is meant to reflect the researcher's interpretation of the participants' experiences, as communicated in the context of the interview setting. By asking participants to comment on additional information in a different context and a different environment (perhaps), this adds an extra dimension to the process, and it should not be surprising if the participants wish to communicate something additional or something different. There are situations where respondent input is valuable, but the nature of this should be carefully considered by the research team.

What should become obvious from reading this section is that attempting to answer these questions without a consideration of your theoretical approach to the research and the specific aim of the research will be very difficult, if not impossible. If your answers are not based on a consistent approach, then you are unlikely to design a project which is consistent. It is this lack of consistency, spawned from a lack of consideration, which is the main reason for qualitative projects not being good enough at final assessment.

It is also worth noting at this point that conducting qualitative research in health-related fields can sometimes result in researcher exposure to potentially distressing information. Qualitative research is intended to take an empathic approach, to build rapport with participants in order to facilitate information exchange, to use the principles of active listening and to ensure (as far as possible) that the well-being of participants is not adversely affected by the research process. In this way, the qualitative research process is similar in some respects to the therapeutic process, and discussions of emotionally intense subjects can develop. It is important, therefore, to ensure that the well-being of researchers is also considered. It is recommended that supervisory meetings should be timetabled into your research proposal with the purpose of attending to your self-care, in the same way that supervisory meetings exist in therapeutic work.

6.2 Collecting qualitative data

The majority of qualitative data collected in health-related research is collected via one-to-one interviews or focus groups. However, there are some novel and interesting methods of collecting qualitative data, and these should be encouraged and developed. My intention in this section is not to present focus groups and interviews as the recommended approach to collecting qualitative data but recognising that one of these methods is the method that most trainee psychologists conducting a qualitative project will adopt, and to present some general guidance about conducting good quality interviews or focus groups.

6.2.1 What makes a good interview?

Interviews designed to collect qualitative data tend to follow a semi-structured approach. That is, they are not completely structured in the sense that there are specific questions that are asked in a specified order, and they are not completely unstructured in the sense that the interviewer does not provide any direction to the interview. Semi-structured interviews fall between these extremes and can differ greatly in the extent to which they are structured. For example, an interviewer may have developed an interview guide containing several main questions which they wish to address in the interview, along with a series of prompts or potential follow-up questions under each main question. The interviewer will adapt the order and wording of the questions according to the participant's responses and might omit some questions or add others depending on the course of the interview. On the other hand, an interviewer might take the approach that it is not possible to know what questions need to be asked from the participants and might begin the interview with one question and then develop questions as the interview continues. This more adaptive approach is commonly found in studies where we know little about the participants, such as in studies of little-known cultures. For understandable reasons, most trainee health and clinical psychologists will tend towards the more structured form of the semi-structured interview. Perhaps this is a result of the trainees (an even their supervisors) being a little anxious about ensuring that the interview produces useful data. It is also reasonable that a more structured interview is conducted by those who are early career qualitative researchers, as the more unstructured interview requires a higher level of skill and comfort with the research interview situation.

The content and structure of your interview will be guided to some extent by your theoretical approach. It is only by reflecting on the purpose of the interview and your theoretical assumptions about the role of the participant and the interviewer in this process that you can decide on the structure of the interview, or on any other data collection method. While we can think of guidelines for the conduct of interviews which primarily aim to collect quantitative data, it is not reasonable to expect a similar set of guidelines for interviews which aim to collect qualitative data, as qualitative research encompasses a range of theoretical approaches. Nevertheless, there are some general principles that are worth considering.

First, it is important to be explicit about the process of the interview. The content and structure of the interview will impact on the data obtained, and you should ensure that the reader of your research can trace how the data was obtained and how this approach was influenced by your theoretical assumptions. Therefore, a clear outline of how you envisage the process in your research proposal is important, as is the detail of how the interview proceeded in reality along with an account of any modifications made to the interview process during the course of the study and why these modifications were thought to be appropriate.

You should also be aware of the context of the interview and how this might influence the data obtained. By context, I mean the environment in which the interview is conducted, the purpose of the interview as perceived by the participant and the interviewer, and the personal situation of the participant. Peripheral events in the environment can distract participants and interviewers, and the environment can create perceptions about the purpose of the interview. For example, an interview conducted in an outpatients' clinic environment immediately after the participant has attended an appointment with their physician could result in a different discussion than an interview conducted in the participant's home. The participant's perception of the purpose of the interview might also be influenced by how it is verbally contextualised by the interviewer. Early in my research career, I collected data for a study examining older people's perceptions of health and social care services that they had received. Although the focus of the study was to collect quantitative data, there was a qualitative element which involved me going to the participants' homes to interview them about their experiences. I was using a (mostly) structured interview schedule, and after a few interviews I began to suspect that I was not getting the full story from participants as everyone seemed very happy with the service they had received, and this contradicted information that I had received from other sources. At the next interview, I deviated a little from the script to try to explore this in more depth, and through discussion with the participant I realised that she believed that I was working on behalf of the health service to check that the care workers had been doing their job effectively. When I explained this was not the case, the participant told me that she had not wanted to make any negative comments about the service 'in case some of those girls lost their job'. It became apparent that it was my initial introduction that created the problem. The unit I worked for had a name which had health and social care in its title, and I used this in my introduction to participants.

They interpreted this as health and social services and believed that I was working for the service provider. This minor miscommunication had a strong influence on the content of the interviews, despite continual reassurances to participants that their responses would be confidential.

When interviewing people with an illness or condition that affects their health (physical or psychological), the stage of the person's journey along the illness trajectory can also influence the outcome of an interview. Again, making this information explicit is essential to aid others' interpretations of your findings and considering this in advance should feed in to your sampling strategy.

If you have experience of conducting one-to-one interviews with clients for assessment and formulation purposes in your clinical work, then don't separate this experience from the research interview. Although these interviews have different purposes, there is some overlap in the skills required. Primarily, it is useful to build a good rapport with participants in both interview situations, and your skill in the clinical situation will help you to achieve this in the research situation. This will be assisted during the course of the interview by demonstrating that the participant is being attended and listened to, by taking an empathic approach to the discussion, by being silent when silence is warranted, and by summarising and probing when further discussion is warranted.

6.2.2 Should I conduct a focus group or interviews?

The first thing to make clear is that focus groups are not group interviews and are not a convenient way of increasing participant numbers without needing to do lots of one-to-one interviews. Focus groups are different from interviews, with a different purpose. The main difference is that in interviews the spotlight is on the data which emanates from a discussion between interviewer and participant; in focus groups, the spotlight is on the data which emanates from the interactions within the group. The discussions that take place in focus groups are fed by the group interaction, and the researcher might be interested not only in the verbal information provided but also in how this information evolved within the group. That is, the discussions, behaviours, and so on, that preceded or occurred alongside the presentation of the verbal information. The researcher's role in a focus group is to facilitate the discussion.

The choice to conduct a focus group rather than interviews, therefore, largely depends on the type of information you are seeking. This includes not only the process by which this information is obtained, but some consideration should be given to the nature of the information sought. For example, is the topic of conversation likely to be one which will be easily discussed in a group – will the group facilitate the conversation or hinder it.

The composition and size of the focus group are also worth considering at the proposal stage of your research. Typically, focus groups of six to ten people are considered optimal, although the specific number will also be determined by the access that you have to the population of potential participants, the time available and the extent of homogeneity desired within each group. The total number of focus groups within a research project is typically three to five, but this will depend on the considerations already outlined, the breadth of the issues to be discussed and the number of times you intend to interview each group (O'Sullivan, 2003, p. 121).

Consider the group composition and the roles that people have within the group. For example, I supervised a clinical psychology trainee who conducted focus groups among cancer survivors to explore their experiences of the effects on their life of surgery to remove the cancer. We sampled the participants from a patient support group and heard very positive stories about their experiences. The research also involved conducting focus groups among the spouses of the cancer survivors. They related a very different story, discussing the negative impact of the surgery and the ongoing anxiety about cancer recurrence. We thought this was a very interesting contrast and wondered why it had arisen. The reason was apparent when we discovered that one of the members of the cancer survivor group had just joined the peer support group after being diagnosed with cancer but had not yet undergone surgery (this person should have been excluded from the study but managed to slip in). Not surprisingly, all the other members of the group adopted their 'support mode', aiming to provide this person with an upbeat, positive message for the future. It was not made explicit in the group, but the presence of this person probably changed the dynamic considerably. In later research, using one-to-one interviews with the cancer survivors, different (more negative) stories about life after surgery were told.

Although some of the skills required to conduct an effective focus group are the same as those required to conduct an effective interview, moderating a focus group requires some additional skills. It is important that you are skilled in managing groups – in working with the group dynamics and ensuring inclusivity in discussions. It is also important that you have good organisational skills, to ensure that a group of people arrive at the same place at the same time, that facilities and refreshments are provided as appropriate, that recording equipment (and any backups) are functional and will have a power supply, and that the discussion remains focused on the general topic of interest.

7

Qualitative Research: Theoretical Approaches

●●●●●●●●●●●●●●●●●●●●●●●●●●●●●●●●●●●●●●

In Chapter 6, I aimed to provide some general guidance about the general issues to be considered when designing and conducting qualitative research. Throughout the previous chapter, I indicated that many of the decisions you make during the course of the qualitative research project will be informed by your theoretical approach to the research. The present chapter aims to address some of the issues which arise for trainee psychologists when studying these theoretical approaches.

This chapter is not intended to be a comprehensive discussion of all theoretical approaches used in qualitative research. Rather it is intended to highlight the main characteristics of some of the theoretical approaches which most commonly drive the qualitative methodologies employed by trainee psychologists. I believe that an overview of these approaches is useful to enable trainees to make a more informed decision about the approach and methodology to be employed in their project. In my experience, health/clinical psychology trainees often begin a qualitative research proposal with a methodology in mind, without having considered the alternatives or the theoretical approach that this methodology stems from. I hope that this chapter will go some way to addressing this problem.

I believe that the best qualitative research proposals are written by trainees who have selected a theoretical approach on the basis of a consideration of some alternatives, selected a methodology which stems from the chosen theoretical approach and then chosen a data collection method which is appropriate to the methodology. For example, a trainee might decide that they wish to adopt a phenomenological approach to their research question; stemming from this, they might choose Interpretative Phenomenological Analysis (IPA) as their method-ology (because they acknowledge the role of the researcher's interpreta-tion in addition to their phenomenological stance) and then opt for a one-to-one interview as an appropriate data collection method which is consistent with the choices made thus far. For me, this represents a logical, considered approach to the research design, and the knowledge that the trainee has developed as a result of thinking through these deci-sions will help to ensure that any decisions made during the course of the research will be consistent with this initial approach. The end result, usually, is a coherent piece of research, and a trainee who can articulate their views clearly and robustly defend their work during a viva and/or in the project report.

Unfortunately, some trainees will start thinking about their data collection method, having found a methodology by chance (in other words, they have chosen a methodology without any consideration of alternatives) and being unaware of the theoretical approach that informs the methodology. For example, some trainees will begin con-versations about their research proposal by saying 'I am doing an IPA study – is it OK to use focus groups?' When I ask them why they have chosen IPA and how it fits with their research question, they develop a worried look, and it becomes clear that they are not really sure why they have chosen this methodology. Perhaps this problem occurs because most trainee psychologists follow an undergraduate pathway which is strong in quantitative research training but not as strong on qualitative research training. Therefore, when choosing a qualita-tive approach for their major research project as part of a training programme, it might be the first time they have undertaken a major qualitative research project. As a result, trainees can sometimes make decisions about their qualitative research without a reasonable appre-ciation of the issues that need to be considered. I need to make it clear at this point that I am not criticising the use of IPA. In fact, I am positively disposed towards IPA (and have co-authored several publica-tions using this methodology). I am making the point that I think it is inappropriate to decide on the specific methodology to be used before considering the research question or the philosophical issues which underpin a methodology.

It is also important to note that there are differences in the litera-ture about what is labelled as a theoretical approach, an epistemology and a methodology. I do not want to spend time debating the differ-ences between these terms, as the aim here is not to get bogged down in philosophical discussions (although some philosophical discussion is inevitable). For the purposes of facilitating a brief overview of common theoretical approaches used in qualitative research, I have made a number of generalisations/assumptions in this chapter:

- By deciding to conduct qualitative research, you have decided that you wish to take a more relativist and less realist epistemological approach to addressing your research question.
- The more relativist side of epistemology includes a number of theoretical approaches, and these have been labelled and categorised in a number of ways.
- Following the distinctions in qualitative research made by Reicher (2000), I have chosen to focus on two theoretical approaches which I believe guide the majority of qualitative research conducted by health/clinical psychology trainees – experiential research, which is primarily guided by phenomenology and discursive research, which is primarily guided by social constructivism.
- Within each theoretical approach, the methodologies commonly used by health/clinical psychology trainees are: grounded theory and interpretative phenomenological analysis (within the experiential approach); and discourse analysis (within the discursive approach). In a survey conducted in 2006, these three methodologies were the most common qualitative methodologies taught on clinical psychology training courses in the UK and the most common qualitative methodologies used by clinical psychology trainees in their major research projects (Harper, in press). It is my belief that the same pattern exists in health psychology training in the UK.

These assumptions may not be held by all qualitative researchers but, in the spirit of qualitative research, I want to make these assumptions clear so that your interpretation of the information I provide is informed. A summary of my assumptions is provided in Table 7.1, although this is a simplistic representation and should be read in conjunction with the information presented in the remainder of this chapter.

7.1 Experiential approaches

The experiential approach to qualitative research is primarily, but not exclusively, driven by a phenomenological tradition. There are methodologies which use an experiential approach and which acknowledge the influences of the social constructivist tradition.

I consider the phenomenological approach to research to refer to the general idea that the aim of research is to develop an understanding

Table 7.1 Contextualising qualitative approaches

Epistemology →	Theoretical approach →	Methodology →	Data collection method
Relativist ↑ ↓ Realist	More Discursive / Social Constructivist More Experiential / Phenomenological Positivist	Discourse Analysis Grounded Theory IPA Experimental	Data collection methods should be flexible, although often include focus groups or one-to-one interviews

of a person's thoughts, feelings and perceptions, in other words, to aim to gain an understanding of an experience from the perspective of the research participant(s). The phenomenological approach suggests that we can seek to develop this understanding by making sense of the research participants' communication about their experiences. In other words, we are seeking to make sense of the participants' interpretations. As such, the phenomenological approach assumes that there is a perceived reality present but that perceptions of reality will differ among individuals, and all perceptions are equally valid, so there are multiple perceived realities. This approach holds that the aim of research is to make sense of the perceived reality of participants and how this is influenced by their assumptions about the world. In doing this, we attempt, as much as possible, to prevent our assumptions about the world from prejudicing our investigation, and we allow findings to emerge which are grounded in the data. To facilitate this, the phenomenological approach generally adopts a systematic, step-by-step treatment of the data to ensure nothing is changed or distorted from its original meaning.

Working with this general approach, it is possible to construct a methodology and conduct a qualitative research project using a general phenomenological framework (see Section 6.1.4.1). This allows the researcher to enjoy the flexibility of the qualitative approach and to develop novel methods of conducting research. However, most trainee psychologists prefer the security of a methodology with some guidelines that can be followed. Although there are obvious benefits to this choice, there is a less obvious drawback. That is, by labelling your research project with a specific methodology, you are placing constraints on how the research can be conducted, and if you step outside these boundaries then your research will not live up to the methodological label you have given it and could be considered poor practice rather than innovative. So if you choose to follow a prescribed methodology, ensure you adhere closely to its principles.

Two different methodologies which can be considered to come under the experiential approach heading are interpretative phenomenological analysis and grounded theory. These are not the only methodologies that we could group under this heading, but are the most commonly used.

7.1.1 What is interpretative phenomenological analysis?

One of the most recently developed and commonly used qualitative methodologies in health and clinical psychology research is interpretative phenomenological analysis (IPA: Smith, 1996). The growth in popularity of the methodology is due, in part, to the clearly articulated guidelines (particularly in comparison to other qualitative approaches) provided by Smith and others for the conduct of studies using IPA, the numerous examples of psychological research relevant to the health-related field, and the network of support for IPA researchers that has developed (www. ipa.bbk.ac.uk).

IPA champions the idiographic approach. In other words, it is focused on the detailed, micro-level examination of individuals. While many IPA studies have been published that include more than one case, the single case study is very much in keeping with the IPA approach. However, the issue is not the number of people in the sample but ensuring that the individual(s) are represented in any reports of the research. Therefore, in IPA studies conducted on a group of people, one would expect to get a sense of the stories of individuals in addition to the themes which emerge from the group. Given the space limitations on journal articles (and in any report of a research project on your training programme), the number of participants that you include in an IPA study should be carefully considered. If you include too many participants, then you might find yourself swamped with data and conducting an analysis which is not true to the IPA approach but is little more than a cursory summary of the participants' responses. As a guide, Turpin et al. (1997) suggest that six to eight participants is an appropriate number for an IPA study conducted for the major research project on a Doctorate in Clinical Psychology training course in the UK. However, more recent papers discussing the IPA approach make a case for smaller sample sizes (Reid, Flowers & Larkin, 2005), including the single case study approach (Eatough & Smith, 2006; Smith, 2004).

As the name suggests, IPA is a phenomenological approach, in that it focuses on the subjective account of a person's experiences and perceptions and seeks to understand how a person makes sense of these experiences. In addition, IPA stems from the position that it is not possible to obtain a true understanding of a person's lived experience and how this is influenced by the person's assumptions about the world, as this understanding will be influenced by the researcher's assumptions about the world and also needs to be placed within the wider social context. Consequently, although the general phenomenological approach is interpretative (in that the research participant is interpreting their experiences and communicating this to the researcher), the interpretative element of IPA refers to the double interpretation (or double hermeneutic) that takes place. That is, the researcher is interpreting the interpretations of the participant. This element of IPA acknowledges the influence of social constructivism, highlighting the problem with 'pigeon-holing' methodologies.

IPA *requires* that the researcher interprets the information provided by the participant, that this is an important part of the sense-making process. A description of the research participant's experience is insufficient in the IPA model, although it might constitute a first order level of analysis. The researcher is obliged to use this data to a fuller extent by attempting to understand the meaning behind the participant's description and their attempts to make sense of their experience. This deeper level analysis might also be informed by psychological constructs and theory.

Given that IPA recognises that the study findings are a product of the researcher's interpretations and encourages (perhaps demands) that the researcher speculates on the meaning behind the participant's interpretations, the findings from an IPA study need to have a clear path from the raw data to the higher order interpretations, so that the reader can trace the interpretations made by the researcher from individual reports. Therefore, a systematic and explicit approach to the analysis of the data is warranted, and this should be detailed in a research proposal. Examples of approaches to the analysis of data in IPA studies are provided in Smith, Jarman & Osborn (1999). You should not underestimate the amount of time required to conduct an analysis of the data in an IPA study. The approach requires you to immerse yourself in the data, to try to get a sense of the perspective of the research participant and to interpret what this means within the wider context. It is important to timetable time for you to reflect on your interpretations of the data and how they have arisen and to revisit these interpretations armed with these reflections.

In my experience, trainee psychologists who undertake a good quality IPA study struggle with what they should do about their analysis. They will regularly revisit the analysis to reframe their interpretations, anxious to ensure that the voice of the research participant(s) is being represented appropriately. Also, they will have difficulty reducing their report of the research to the word length imposed by external authorities, as removing or reducing bits of information from the report distorts the picture and does not fully represent the information provided by participant(s), in the opinion of the trainees. To a large extent, these struggles are a positive indication that the trainee has developed a sense of the research participant's experiences and wants to ensure that others develop a similar understanding; the trainee is passionate about conveying the stories of the individuals in their research. This is commensurate with the philosophy of IPA and is not something I want to discourage. I draw your attention to it simply because if you are conducting an IPA study and you become involved with the data at a deeper level, you will need to leave time at the end of the process to gradually allow yourself to convert your information into meaningful summaries which retain the essence of the individual and the important elements of your interpretations. In other words, the write-up of an IPA study is part of your personal journey through this research process and takes time.

An example of a trainee psychologist's completed research project, using an IPA methodology can be found in Hill, Higgins, Dempster and McCarthy (2009). This research was conducted by a trainee clinical psychologist, and the published version is very similar to the research report submitted by the trainee as part of her training programme.

7.1.2 What is grounded theory?

Grounded Theory actually refers to the outcome of a study using a particular methodology. That is, we develop a grounded theory through undertaking a specific course of research. Nevertheless, the process by which we derive a grounded theory has now come to be known as grounded theory – the methodology has been labelled by its outcome.

A grounded theory methodology is a way of conducting research which aims to use qualitative data to generate a theory, which is grounded in the data. The classical grounded theory approach was developed by Glaser and Strauss (1967). This initial exposition of grounded theory was embedded in a phenomenological, critical realist approach but there have been deviations from this approach over the years, which has resulted in disagreements about what is accurately described as grounded theory and the extent to which it should be situated in a phenomenological approach (as opposed to a social constructivist approach). Indeed, even the original proponents of grounded theory have disagreed about the epistemological underpinnings of this methodology (Strauss & Corbin, 1990; Glaser, 1992).

The aim of grounded theory is to develop a theory which has been generated by the data. Therefore there is an onus on the researcher to attempt to prevent their preconceptions and theoretical knowledge from influencing the generation of this theory. Often, this is assumed to mean that the researcher should avoid reading any of the published literature in the area and should avoid formulating specific research questions. It is highly unlikely that you will be able to direct your research project appropriately and complete it in time by adopting this approach. There is nothing wrong with developing a research question for a grounded theory study which has been informed by your knowledge of the literature. Grounded theory indicates that it is inappropriate for this knowledge to influence the generation of the theory rather than the theory being generated by the data. Therefore, the researcher is required to reflect on how their theory is developing and the extent to which it is grounded in the data. This is particularly important at the later stages of the study, when the theoretical concepts are becoming more abstract and your knowledge of the field will be useful in helping to clarify the theory. This is known as theoretical sensitivity.

In a grounded theory approach, the theory is developed through an iterative process of collecting and interrogating the data until theoretical saturation has been reached. In other words, data collection and data analysis proceed concurrently and will influence each other. The data collected will be examined and categorised, and hypotheses will be formulated about these categories and how they relate to each other. This will guide the sampling procedure which will provide further data to test the hypotheses formulated and raise further questions about the relationships between the data which can then be addressed through further purposive sampling, leading to the development and/or modification of hypotheses. This iterative process continues until a theory has been established which is based in the data and which is not being modified (but is being confirmed) by the addition of further data.

The process of conducting a grounded theory study is not a linear one. The iterative nature of the methodology can sometimes make you feel that you are no closer to developing your theory than when you started. It is like travelling towards a point in the distance. If you fix your sights on the destination, it seems like you are making little progress, and it is only when you look back at your starting point that you realise how far you have travelled and it is only when you look at points closer to you that you realise how quickly you are moving. Therefore, although you should not lose sight of your end goal – the development of your theory – you also need to let the data guide you to the more immediate questions that need to be resolved, building towards more abstract theoretical concepts. Chamberlain (1999) helpfully describes three phases of the grounded theory study:

1. *Open sampling and open coding.* This is the initial data collection and analysis phase. Data from the first purposively selected participants is tentatively coded into categories.
2. *Relational or variational sampling and axial (focused) coding.* In this phase, participants are selected purposively to enable the elaboration of categories and identify the nature and limitations of the relationships between them. New categories might also be identified at this phase, which will require this phase to be revisited for these new categories.
3. *Discriminate sampling and selective coding.* Purposive sampling to confirm the theory that has been developed and demonstrate saturation. In this phase, the core category of the theory is identified and related to other categories. The core category is the single, superordinate category which is central to the theory generated.

Again, it should be emphasised that this is not a linear process but an example of how a grounded theory study might proceed. The common elements of a grounded theory approach are the existence of theoretical sampling until theoretical saturation and a constant comparative method – data is being collected and compared with existing data on an ongoing basis. It should be obvious that engaging in this process requires the handling of a great deal of information, not just categories of data but how these relate to each other and coincide to form a core category. Therefore, you need a strategy for managing the data. Diagrams are useful and commonly used in grounded theory studies, and you might also want to consider using a qualitative data analysis computer package to organise your information.

One of the most common questions asked by trainees about grounded theory research is how to know when you have generated a good theory. In general terms, a theory is good if it fits and if it works. In other words, the theory should be plausible and provide a recognisable description of the phenomenon. This will occur if the theory is faithful to the data; if the data are comprehensive enough to include adequate variation, thereby allowing it to be applicable to a range of contexts, if the limits of applicability are clear, if the interpretation of the data is comprehensive, and if the theory can be used by those working in the area.

Some examples of grounded theory studies relevant to health and clinical psychology can be found in Timlin-Scalera, Ponterotto, Blumberg and Jackson (2003); López, Eng, Randall-David and Robinson (2005), and Noiseux and Ricard (2008).

7.2   Discursive approaches

Discursive approaches to qualitative research can be considered to fall within a social constructivist epistemology. Social constructivism is part of the wider constructivist epistemological tradition. Social constructivism assumes that the researcher cannot be separated from the participant. In other words, the researcher does not gather data from a participant which represents that participant's experiences. Rather the researcher plays a role in constructing the data as the data is a product of the inter-action between the researcher and participant. The researcher is part of the life-world experienced by the research participant.

Social constructivism posits that there is no single reality that can be studied but that 'reality' is what an individual constructs through their interaction with the world. There is a subtle but important difference here between social constructivism and phenomenology. In phenomenology, there is an implicit notion that a reality does exist, although individuals will perceive reality in different ways and it is these perceptions which are the focus of phenomenology. In social constructivism, the assumption is that reality is specific to the individual, and, therefore, there are multiple realities. The focus is on how these realities are socially constructed by individuals and groups.

The social constructivist approach is that the world (that is, meanings in our life-world) does not need to be as it is at present, as the present is a social construction. Different social constructions will be developed at different points in time and by different cultures and so meaning is a dynamic process. Therefore, how things are in the world does not exist independent of the thoughts of the people in the world. Consequently, to explore someone's experience is to influence the social construction of this experience. Furthermore, information provided by a research participant about their experience is affected by and reflects this process of social constructivism. Therefore, research is a process of trying to interpret the communications of research participants to make sense of their constructions of meaning.

There are a number of methodologies that use this approach. The most commonly used of these in health/clinical psychology is discourse analysis.

7.2.1   What is discourse analysis?

Discourse analysis is the study of language in naturally occurring social settings, with a focus on what the language reveals about that social situation. Discourse analysis posits that language is not necessarily a reflection of underlying thoughts and feelings and is not descriptive of the person's life-world. Rather meanings are actively constructed in social interaction through the use of language. Therefore, language is inseparable from the social context. For example, different language is used in different social contexts – when discussing your opinions about your training programme, you are likely to use different language when this discussion takes place during a coffee break and only involves other trainees compared with when this discussion takes place in a course committee meeting with course staff.

Discourse analysis is a generic term, and there are a number of methodologies that can be delineated with this general heading, which are influenced by different disciplines within the broad social sciences. Of particular interest to psychologists are the approaches labelled as discursive psychology and Foucauldian discourse analysis.

Foucauldian discourse analysis is concerned with language as a product. This type of discourse analysis deconstructs the language used by people to discern how this language has meaning within the socio-cultural context. In other words, what discursive resources are available to people and how they became available and how they influence identity, ideology and social change. Sometimes a Foucauldian discourse analysis will chart the construction of a phrase in the historical context. For example, Heaton (1999) discusses the development of discourse of the 'informal carer' by examining texts from health and social policy documents in the UK. In other cases, this approach can be used to examine the role of language in positioning of the participant or by the participant within the discourse. An example of this type of approach in exploring talk about dietary management among people with recently diagnosed Type 2 Diabetes is provided by Peel, Parry, Douglas & Lawton (2005). They found that talk was constructed to provide complex reasons for non-compliance with dietary management guidelines by participants, in an attempt to present themselves in a positive light. The paper presents a discussion about why the participants are motivated to present themselves in this way and how this is influenced by the social context, and queries the notion and value of the term 'compliance'.

Discursive psychology focuses on the functions of language and how these functions are achieved. It can be considered more radical in its constructivist assumptions than Foucauldian discourse analysis. Discursive psychology is interested in the process of how things are constructed through the use of language – how people use language and what this language is intended for. Discursive psychologists aim to identify the discursive strategies (or patterns of discourse) used to accomplish social actions. For example, Horton-Salway (2001) demonstrates how a discursive psychology approach was used to examine talk about personal accountability in myalgic encephalomyelitis (ME). This study provides a useful discussion of how attributions are constructed by people with ME as part of an interaction to manage blame and personal accountability. Horton-Salway suggests that illness attributions should not be seen as stable characteristics but as a product of an interaction which aims to accomplish a certain task within the social context.

There are those who consider the segmentation and differential labelling of discourse analytic approaches to be unhelpful as it makes the general approach appear inaccessible and discourages researchers from exploring ways of using discourse analytic techniques. Therefore, a more general discourse analysis approach, which attempts to allow for different variants has been suggested (Wetherell, 1998).

The stages of analysis of discourse analysis can seem quite intensive and time consuming and are not always described clearly in texts in the area. Partly, this is due to the fact that discourse analysis is a broad term rather than a single, specific, narrowly defined methodology. Nevertheless, this can also make the approach appear inaccessible to novel researchers and so the attempt by Potter and Wetherell (1987) to provide guidelines for discourse analysis is welcomed. You might also like to consider the reflections of trainee psychologists and their supervisor on using discourse analysis for their major research project (Harper, O'Connor, Self & Stevens, 2008).

8

Evaluating Psychological Services

● ●

According to the British Psychological Society (BPS) accreditation guidelines for clinical psychology training programmes, clinical psychology trainees, undertaking a training course accredited by the BPS, are required to conduct a 'small-scale project involving the use of audit, service development, service evaluation or applied research methods within a clinical placement setting'. Similar projects might be conducted by health psychology trainees as part of a project to demonstrate competence in consultancy. Furthermore, such research is an essential part of the work of clinical and health psychologists to assure quality in their service. This chapter aims to highlight the problems and solutions with conducting research in a service context. It will also discuss the distinction between research, service evaluation and audit and the implications of these differences for obtaining ethics approval. The chapter will, additionally, attempt to outline some research designs which may be useful and appropriate for service evaluation/audit but which are considered less acceptable for more rigorous research.

8.1   Service-related projects vs research projects

The quote in the opening paragraph of this chapter refers to a 'small-scale project'. In my view, this is a misnomer. Talking about small-scale projects with trainees can lead to the erroneous belief that the difference between this project and the 'large-scale' or 'major' project is the sample size. In other words, trainees develop a notion that a small-scale project is research conducted with a small sample and a large-scale project, or their main research project, should be conducted with a large sample. This is not the case and is detrimental in terms of promoting good quality case studies and small n designs as an appropriate research study for the main research project.

I prefer the term 'service-related project' rather than 'small-scale project', although that option is also not completely free of ambiguity. Whatever term is used, it is clear that the difference between the service-related project and the major research project is not sample size, which leads us to our first question.

8.1.1   What is the difference between the service-related project and the major research project?

The main difference between these projects is the purpose of the project. For the major research project, the primary purpose is to contribute to the psychological knowledge base in such a way that a particular area of interest is advanced. Therefore, the conclusions of the research project must be of interest to psychologists (and others) because these conclusions help in the further understanding of an issue by, for example, advancing theory or improving methodology. Consequently, conclusions which are limited to the sample under investigation are unlikely to be sufficient for your main research project.

For the service-related project, the primary purpose is to contribute to the development of a specific service. As a result, the service-related project tends to have a more local focus than the main research project. A potentially useful method of considering whether a project might be appropriate for a service-related project is to ask yourself what types of recommendation you will be able to make to the service after the project has been completed, regardless of the findings. If the answer is not obvious, then perhaps your project is not sufficiently service related.

Of course, it is possible for a service-related project and a research project to look very similar. That is, it is possible for good quality, rigorous research to be conducted which also results in useful recommendations for a specific service. Therefore, it is not necessarily the design or methods which make a project service related, but the purpose and aim of the project.

The BPS definition specifically mentions audit, service development and service evaluation, and, in my experience, these are the types of projects which most often constitute a service-related project. So it is worth looking at these types of projects in a little more detail.

An audit is a project which aims to assess current practice within a service and whether this practice meets appropriate standards. For example, a service might be keen to conduct an audit of their referrals. This audit might examine whether referrals are made to the service in line with the referral criteria, whether the people making the referrals are appropriate and whether the referrals are dealt with according to the specified procedures and within the specified time limit. Often an audit is a document-based project (for example, extracting information from case notes or computerised monitoring systems), although the collection of qualitative data via focus groups or interviews can also be useful. Audits can be perceived to be threatening by staff depending on how their findings are used by managers, so careful negotiation with staff about the purpose and the parameters of any audit you are involved in is important.

Service development is a broad term which refers to any work which helps a service to develop and improve. Audit and service evaluation will feed in to service development. Another type of project which will help services develop appropriately is a needs assessment. A psychological needs assessment is an assessment of the types of the psychological needs of a specific population, which will help to build a case for the development of a psychological service to meet these needs. For example, a psychological needs assessment might conduct a survey of all patients within an area who have heart disease. The survey might ask these people about the state of their psychological health, the type of psychosocial problems they encounter and what sort of help they would like in dealing with these problems. If the information indicates a strong need and desire for psychological support among the population, then this can form part of a business case for the development of psychological services in this area.

Service evaluation aims to determine whether a psychological service has been effective in meeting its goals. Often there is an emphasis on outcomes – that is to what extent the people who have received the service experience the intended outcome. For example, a service evaluation of a smoking cessation service might focus on recording the proportion of people receiving the service who have stopped smoking and the proportion of people receiving the service who have reduced the amount of cigarettes they smoke. However, a good service evaluation will also examine the process that led to these outcomes to determine the elements of the service that are effective. For example, there might be an investigation of the aspects of the smoking cessation intervention that the clients found most and least helpful.

8.1.2 Do service-related projects require ethics approval?

Let me clarify that when trainees ask this question, they are usually referring to the requirement for formal ethics approval as outlined in Section 3.3. I am assuming that you will be familiar with the ethical principles that all psychological research should conform to, and you will be aware of your professional obligations to ensure a high standard of ethical practice in everything that you do. I am also assuming that the institution in which you undertake your training programme might have some internal procedures to be followed regarding ethical approval for a service-related project. Therefore, I will restrict this answer to the requirement for formal, NHS ethics approval.

Unfortunately, there is no clear answer to this question. The NHS National Research Ethics Service (NRES) provides some guidance about the definition of research, which requires formal ethics approval, and service evaluation or audit, which does not (NRES, 2009). If your research clearly falls into one definition or the other, then the decision about proceeding for ethics approval is relatively straightforward (see Box 8.1). However, be aware that the service/trust in which your service-related project is being conducted may require the project proposal to be approved by an audit committee, or some similar body, in situations where formal ethical approval is not being sought. So it is important to make yourself aware of any local arrangements of this nature.

Box 8.1   Defining research for NRES ethics approval

Guidance from NRES (2009) highlights four criteria which will help researchers to discriminate between research that requires formal ethical approval and service evaluation/audit which does not require formal ethical approval from NRES. These are:

1. *Intent*. The primary aim of research is to develop generalisable new knowledge. The primary aim of audit/service evaluation is to measure standards of care.
2. *Treatment/service*. Audit or service evaluation does not use an intervention without a firm basis of support. In other words, research might include the evaluation of a novel intervention in order to test whether this intervention works; service evaluation involves testing an intervention where there is already support for its implementation (that is, it is already in use or about to be implemented and is not being implemented for the purposes of the service evaluation).
3. *Allocation*. In audit/service evaluation, patients receive treatment/ service based on a joint decision by the clinician and the patient. Patients are never allocated to a treatment/service on the basis of a protocol, as is often the case in research.
4. *Randomisation*. It follows from the previous point that if randomisation is used, it is research.

In reality, the guidance provided by NRES and the BPS do not and could not cover all eventualities, and often it is not clear to a trainee whether their service-related project should be considered as 'research' or 'service evaluation/audit', as defined by NRES. The assistance of your supervisor will be helpful in working through this decision. If in doubt, seek clarification from your local NHS Trust Research Office or NHS Research Ethics Committee (REC). However, bear in mind that this will extend the timetable for your project, especially if formal ethical approval is required.

In formal training programmes, the time allocated for the conduct of the service-related project often precludes the possibility of obtaining formal ethics approval from NRES. Therefore, regardless of your ambitions, your project might be restricted to one which conforms to the definition of audit or service evaluation, as defined by NRES.

8.2 Balancing scientific rigour with practicability

As mentioned previously, service-related projects can be examples of good quality research projects. However, in my experience of clinical psychology training programmes this is usually not the case. This is not to say that these service-related projects have been carried out in a haphazard manner or that they are not worthwhile projects. In fact, the opposite is true. In my experience, service-related projects often begin with a project proposal which conforms closely to the research proposal (see Section 3.2). This proposal is carefully considered and scrutinised (and is necessary to ensure that all relevant parties are informed about the aims and parameters of the project), and the project is then conducted in a systematic, considered manner. When I suggest that service-related projects are often not examples of good quality research projects, I am not suggesting that they are poor quality projects, but rather that they do not conform to the quality criteria that we would expect from a research project (as discussed in Section 4.1). In fact, one could argue that to compare a service-related project with a research project is an unfair comparison – they are separate and distinct pieces of work with different aims, and, therefore, there is no reason to expect that one would be similar to the other (although sometimes they are).

Service-related projects often do not conform to the criteria associated with good quality research because of the aim of the projects. Primarily, service-related projects aim to inform a local service by providing information which will contribute to the development of that service. Therefore, characteristics such as random sampling that we would like to see in a research project are not necessary in a service-related project. In addition, service-related projects will often aim to examine the outcomes for the people who are receiving this particular service/treatment. The focus of the project will not necessarily be on the efficacy of the service in relation to a no treatment comparison (or some other comparison), but on the effectiveness of the treatment as it was delivered in a clinical setting. Therefore, characteristics such as random allocation of participants to comparison and treatment groups that we would like to see in a research project are not always necessary in a service-related project. Furthermore, the introduction of some of these design characteristics would result in a service-related project being defined as research for the purposes of NRES ethical approval, which would add a considerable time investment to the project. Consequently, the design of the service-related project needs to be considered carefully to ensure that it meets its aim in as rigorous a manner as possible, in light of the various constraints.

8.2.1   How can I evaluate service outcomes without allocating participants to different groups?

In Chapter 4, I emphasised the importance of ensuring that a research design maximises internal validity, if you wish to make cause-and-effect conclusions about an intervention. Therefore, if you wish to evaluate the effect that a service has on the outcomes for clients, it makes sense to formulate a research design which will minimise threats to internal validity. Important design characteristics which help to achieve this are the inclusion of a control (or comparison) group and the use of random allocation to the intervention and control groups. However, the inclusion of a control (or comparison) group is often not possible or practicable within the context of a service evaluation. A service evaluation aims to evaluate the effectiveness of a service as it is delivered, so any modification of existing service protocols, which guide the clients' access to the service would create a level of artificiality that would prevent the service evaluation from achieving its aim and, in some circumstances, could be considered unethical. The upshot is that a different research design is required – one which recognises a reduction in internal validity based on practical constraints.

At first, this compromise might feel a little uncomfortable – you might wonder about the value of conducting a service evaluation which does not have high internal validity. To reassure yourself that the evaluation is still worthwhile, spend a little time considering the notion of internal validity and what its purpose is. Ensuring that a research design has high internal validity is a way of controlling any variables that might influence the outcomes in your study, so that you can be sure that when the outcomes in your study change, this change is most likely caused by the intervention. In other words, studies high in internal validity help us to identify the things that change outcomes for people so that this information can help to inform theory and can help others to establish similar interventions. But a service evaluation does not aim to inform theory and does not aim to inform others about how to establish a similar intervention – the information generated is primarily for consumption by stakeholders in the service.

A common design used in service evaluations is the one group pre-test post-test design. Simply, this is what a randomised controlled trial might look like if the control group was removed. It involves measuring the outcomes of interest among clients prior to them receiving the intervention and then measuring these outcomes again after the intervention has ended. Variations on this design can be used by adding more data collection points. For example, outcomes could be assessed at a midpoint in the time frame of the intervention and/or outcomes could be assessed at a later follow-up point some time after the intervention has ended. Nevertheless, the pre-test (before delivery of the intervention) and post-test (after delivery of the intervention) time points are key, as the difference between the outcome measures assessed at these time points is an indication of the effect of the intervention. As there is no control group, we cannot be sure that any changes noted are a direct result of the intervention but clinically significant improvements in outcomes strongly suggest that the intervention is worthwhile. Of course, it would be very useful to know what specific aspects of the service were most likely to have caused the changes identified within the service evaluation, and this can be assessed by addressing this question directly with service providers and clients (often involving the collection of qualitative data).

8.2.2   Can I examine the service delivery rather than outcomes?

In broad terms, many service-related projects fall into two categories: those that focus on the outcomes of the service and those that focus on the process. The service evaluation design mentioned above focuses on the outcomes of the service and is important to ensure that clients who receive a service experience the outcomes that service providers should expect. The following examples are types of service-related projects that focus on the process. This is not an exhaustive list. Indeed, the most interesting, and often most informative, service-related projects that I have read have included something novel in the project design. I encourage you to spend some time thinking about something innovative that you could bring to a service-related project.

8.2.2.1 Assessing client satisfaction

Clients' satisfaction with a service is an indication of the clients' experience with the service delivery. An assessment of client satisfaction might encompass the client's overall experience of all aspects of the service, or it might focus on a specific element of the service, for example, the client's satisfaction with their experience of being on the waiting list for the service or the client's satisfaction with the facilities in which the service was provided.

A simple assessment of client satisfaction involves asking clients to complete a questionnaire in which they are asked to rate their satisfaction with the service (or specific aspects of the service). However, this approach is too simplistic and will provide information which is not useful in terms of service development. A more informative assessment of client satisfaction will aim to identify the aspects of the service which could be improved rather than simply stating the percentage of 'satisfied customers'. This will require the careful design of an appropriate questionnaire and/or the collection of qualitative data. Carr-Hill (1992) provides a useful discussion of the issues that need to be considered with this type of project.

8.2.2.2 Auditing referral patterns

An audit assesses whether current practice meets appropriate standards. Service-related projects will sometimes audit whether current referral patterns to a psychological service are appropriate. This type of project helps to inform service providers about whether their referral guidelines need to be revised to reduce/prevent future inappropriate referrals.

Often, psychological services have a very specific remit, and the funding provided to the service will not allow the service to broaden this remit. That is, the service will be constrained in terms of the type of intervention it can provide and in terms of the type of client that it can accept. Referrals are often made to psychological services by other health professionals, and, therefore, these other health professionals need to be made aware of the parameters of the service. It is common practice to provide potential referrers with a set of referral guidelines, which usually consist of a set of criteria that a client needs to meet before they are deemed appropriate for referral to the specific service. However, sometimes it can be difficult to provide concise referral criteria for a psychological service. For example, let's say a health psychology service has been established with the remit of addressing diabetes-related health behaviour difficulties among people with Type 1 Diabetes. In other words, the health psychologist is being funded to engage in therapeutic work with people with

Type 1 Diabetes who present with self-management issues such as insulin omission, no blood sugar testing, lack of dietary control and so on. The health psychologist is not being funded to work with people with Type 1 Diabetes who only present with emotional issues, such as people who are anxious about future complications that might result from their diabetes. Therefore, to accept referrals of people who fall in to this latter group would mean that the psychologist's waiting list would grow, yet they would not be fulfilling the aim of the service. In this case, it is important for the psychologist to inform the other members of the diabetes team about the type of patients that should be referred. The problem is that self-management behavioural issues often coincide with emotional difficulties – a patient might be anxious about future complications because their blood sugar levels are always high because they omit their insulin, for example. So writing clear and concise criteria that can be applied by non-psychologists and that will result only in appropriate referrals is difficult. In fact, the establishment of referral criteria is a process which needs to be audited so that it can be improved over time, as other health professionals' understanding of the service and the psychologist's understanding of the other health professionals' perceptions develops.

The key issue in conducting an audit of referral patterns is the definition of an appropriate and inappropriate referral. This is not always obvious from an examination of the referral criteria (if it was, then inappropriate referrals would be unlikely). Therefore, it is important to spend some time with the service providers to establish what they consider to be appropriate referrals and developing clear criteria for this. Indeed, this might be a useful exercise in itself which will feed into your recommendations about how the referral criteria could be revised.

8.2.2.3 Psychological needs assessment

A needs assessment for a psychological service is usually conducted at the planning stage of the establishment of a service or as part of the desire to develop/augment a service. Needs assessments are used to indicate the level of need among a specified population for a particular psychological service. A needs assessment can be conducted in a specific or non-specific manner. A specific needs assessment aims to identify the specific issues that potential clients of the service most wish to see addressed in the service. A non-specific assessment aims to provide a general indication of the levels of psychological health/ill-health within a specified population.

Service providers can use the information from a non-specific needs assessment to make a case for the provision of a psychological service in an area where one does not exist. For example, if a survey of people with heart disease within a specified area indicates high levels of psychological distress among this population, this information will support any bids for funding to establish a psychological service for people with heart disease. This type of assessment might also be useful in targeting the proposed intervention. For example, it might become clear from analysis of the data that it is mostly men who are experiencing high levels of emotional distress and that this distress manifests as symptoms of depression. A more specific area of high need is thereby identified.

A non-specific needs assessment will help service providers to tailor their service to meet the specific requirements of their potential clients. Often, this type of assessment is conducted when a service is already established, but it can also be conducted at the planning stage of a service. In fact, combining a specific and non-specific assessment can provide a comprehensive picture of needs.

Needs assessments that will inform the development of psychological services can also be conducted among other health professionals. The development of a psychological service can be helpfully informed by the views of other professionals about the type of service that they perceive a need for and would like to be able to refer patients to.

An example of a comprehensive psychological needs assessment which argues the case for the establishment of a psychological service among people with diabetes is provided in Malone, Dempster & Davies (2005).

8.3   Characteristics of a good quality service-related project

Where possible, the characteristics of a good quality research project should be considered to apply to a service-related project. However, given that a research project and a service-related project have different aims, there will be some differences in what constitutes a good quality research project and what constitutes a good quality service-related project. The threats to internal validity in research designs outlined in Chapter 4 should be addressed in a service-related project, where possible. However, the lack of a control group in a service-related project will mean that minimising threats to internal validity will be difficult. In terms of external validity (as discussed in Chapter 4), the ecological validity of service-related projects is usually high, but the population validity is likely to be low, as service-related projects usually employ some type of convenience sampling.

8.3.1 What are the indicators of quality in the design of a service-related project?

As with research projects, the time spent considering the design of a service-related project is time well spent. Chapter 3 provides a discussion of issues that should be considered when designing a research project. The discussions in Chapter 3 about the feasibility of a research idea apply equally when considering the feasibility of a service-related project, and I encourage you to revisit this section of Chapter 3.

Additionally, when conducting a service-related project, the following issues are important to address at the design stage:

- *Clarify the parameters of the project.* You should obtain agreement between all parties involved in the project about the aims/objectives of the project, the responsibilities of everyone involved, the nature of the final report that will be delivered and the timetable for the project. This should be written down and could be provided in the format of a contract (in the case of health psychology trainees undertaking a service-related project as a consultancy project, a contract is necessary).
- *Understand the service context.* If you are to conduct any type of evaluation of a service, it is important to understand the context in which this service operates. This includes how the service is linked to other services, the historical development of the service, the current pressures on the service and the perceived rationale for the project you are about to undertake. Without this information, any recommendations you make to the service, on the basis of your data, run the risk of being ill informed and potentially problematic for the service providers. The aim of your project should not simply be to identify problems but to work with the service to identify solutions. However, part of your discussions with the service team at the outset of the planning stage of the project should be a consideration of potential negative consequences that might result from the proposed project and how these should be handled, with the understanding that it would be inappropriate to suppress negative findings for a service simply because they are negative.
- *Identify appropriate assessment methods.* When conducting research projects, the choice of appropriate assessment methods is crucial to the quality of the information obtained in the study. The same applies to service-related projects. Issues such as reliability, validity, sensitivity and feasibility should be considered. Furthermore, in the case of service evaluations, it is important to consider whether

the outcome measures chosen are appropriate for the intervention to be evaluated. For example, if evaluating a psychological service which aims to alleviate symptoms of depression among clients, it would seem that choosing any reliable, valid and sensitive questionnaire that purports to measure depression would be appropriate. However, there are several questionnaires that claim to measure depression, and they all use different items. Choosing a questionnaire after a careful scrutiny of the types of questions asked and how this matches with the type of intervention and intended effects of the intervention will help to ensure that the intervention is evaluated appropriately.

8.3.2 What are the indicators of quality in the report of a service-related project?

The report of a service-related project often follows the conventional structure of a research project (introduction, method, results, discussion), and the type of information included in a service-related project report is similar to that included in a research project report (see Chapter 9). Nevertheless, there are some characteristics of a good quality service-related project report that you would not necessarily find in a research project report:

- *A description of the service.* As a specific service is being evaluated, the nature and context of this service should be described in the report.
- *A focus on effect sizes.* Service-related projects often involve small samples. Where the analysis of quantitative data is undertaken with small samples, this can limit the value of inferential statistical tests (see Section 5.3). Furthermore, in service-related projects, the aim is usually not to make inferences about the sample to some larger population, but to explore the sample data for its own value. When these situations apply, the analysis of the data should focus on effect sizes rather than on statistical significance – the focus should be on describing the size of any effects found and interpreting these effects in terms of their clinical significance. These effect sizes might be effect sizes for a group or could be reports of effects at the individual level.
- *A cost analysis.* Services operate in a competitive resource environment, and it is important that resources are used efficiently. A good quality service-related project will acknowledge this and, in addition to providing information about service outcomes and/or process,

will also consider the cost implications of the service. Ideally, a cost-effectiveness analysis would be conducted as part of any service evaluation but this is not always possible, partly because the information needed for such an analysis is not always available or obtainable and partly because the skills of a health economist are required to assist with this analysis. Nevertheless, some type of cost analysis might be possible. At a simple level, this means identifying the cost of the service and comparing this with the potential savings that are accrued from the outcomes of the service. For example, the cost of a health psychology service that deals with self-management issues among people with diabetes and results in a reduction in HbA1c levels among clients of the service could be compared with the cost of dealing with people with diabetes who have recurring high HbA1c levels (such as inpatient hospital stays for ketoacidosis, more frequent follow-up review appointments with a diabetic specialist nurse, medication and further treatment to deal with complications, and so on).

• *Recommendations for the service.* The primary aim of a service-related project is to provide information to a service which will allow an informed consideration of future service development. A good way of illustrating that your project meets this aim is to provide a list of recommendations for the service, based on the findings presented in your project. In effect, this is simply a summary of the clinical applications of your findings, but I think that when they are worded as recommendations, they make the application more obvious. It should follow that if producing a set of recommendations is a good way of demonstrating that you have fulfilled the requirement of a service-related project, then during the design stage of your project, considering the types of recommendation that you might be able to make when the project is completed is a useful method of determining whether your project is truly service related.

9

Research Write-up, Viva and Dissemination

● ●

When you get to this stage of the research process, you might feel like the bulk of the work is over. That is true, but there is still some important work to be done. My research supervisor in my first paid research post told me that a research project is not completed until the findings are disseminated. There are many reasons, ethical and scientific in nature, why this is true, but the most motivating rationale for me is as follows. Psychological research in health or clinical psychology should be worthwhile; it should aim to make a difference to people's lives; it should aim to make things better for people. This seems like a lofty aim, but I believe that this type of psychological research should strive to achieve this aim, even in a small and indirect way. If you cannot make the link between your research and how things might improve for people, then I wonder why you are doing the research. People who like to count things refer to this as impact and try to quantify it. I don't support this approach to the assessment of research, but I do think that you should know how your research might make an 'impact'. I am confident that, in my experience, the substantial majority of research projects conducted by trainee psychologists meet this aim. Therefore, generating findings that (even in a small and indirect manner) have the potential to make things better for people and then keeping these findings to yourself (or within your own research team) is, I believe, unacceptable. Research findings need to be disseminated among the people who are most likely to find them useful.

When undertaking a research project as part of a qualification, this requirement does not disappear, but it is probably only part of the dissemination process. For most health or clinical psychology trainees, dissemination of the research project will involve the presentation of a final written report for assessment, perhaps an oral examination (viva) and the publication of the research report for consumption by an appropriate external audience. I will discuss each of these elements in more detail.

9.1 Writing a research report

It is always disappointing to see a good research project suffering at the assessment stage because it is not presented well. Unfortunately, sometimes trainees do not allocate the amount of time to writing up their research report that they need to ensure that it is presented in a way that reflects the quality of the research conducted. I strongly urge you not to rush this part of the research process. Writing up the research is important, and sufficient time needs to be set aside to allow you to do your work justice. Time should be allocated to complete a draft of the report and then allow time for your supervisor to read the draft and provide feedback and for you to incorporate this feedback into your final submission.

The information presented in this section aims to provide general guidelines about writing a research report and also to address more specific issues about submitting a research report for publication in a peer-reviewed journal.

9.1.1 How should I structure my research report?

There is some variation between training programmes in terms of the requirements for the structure and format of a final research report. The main difference is that some programmes will expect the research report to be submitted in the format of a research paper to be published in a peer-reviewed journal, and other programmes will expect the research report to be submitted in the format of a lengthier dissertation. Therefore, it is important to check with your supervisor about the specific requirements for your training programme. My intention here is to provide some guidance about the generic structure of a research report. This guidance should be read in conjunction with any specific guidance provided by your training programme.

Research reports are commonly structured using the following headings: Introduction, Method, Results, Discussion. The Introduction section should provide the context and background for the research project. It should be a discussion of previous research in the area or any relevant related research which helps us to understand the issue under examination. The Introduction section should also provide a discussion of any theoretical framework which underpins the research. This section should be written in such a way that it highlights the gap in the previous research that justifies the need for your research and indicates how your research would advance knowledge in the area. The Introduction section normally ends with a statement of the research questions/hypotheses. In principle, the Introduction section could be written before data collection begins. In fact, you will have completed a similar section in your research proposal (see Chapter 3), and this will likely form the basis of the Introduction section in your final report. If submitting a research report in a dissertation format, your Introduction section will probably discuss previous research in greater detail than would be found in a journal article. Therefore, you might wish to use subheadings within this section, to provide a clearer structure.

The Method section of your research report will also be based on your research proposal, although in your research report the Method section is written in the past tense, whereas in your proposal, this information is written in the future tense. It is possible that during the research process, not everything proceeded as planned and some minor amendments needed to be made to the research proposal. The Method section in your final report should detail what happened rather than what you thought might happen. Usually, a Method section will contain the following information:

- The number of participants approached, the number who refused, the number who did not complete the study, and the final number of participants who completed the study and on whom the analyses are based.
- The research materials/instruments used, information on their psychometric properties and/or justification for the content of these instruments.
- The procedure by which participants were sampled and recruited.
- The design of the research and procedures followed by the participants during the study.

Sometimes a Method section will conclude with a subsection on the methods of analysis. This subsection contains information on how the data was treated in the study and what procedures/tests were used to answer the research questions.

A Results section contains the results of the data analyses. When dealing with quantitative data, a Results section will be a presentation of each analysis in text, table or graph form. The information is usually presented without discussion – you are simply providing the reader with the results, and your discussion of these is left for the next section of the report. Each analysis should be clearly linked to a research question. When dealing with qualitative data, the research findings are sometimes presented in conjunction with a discussion of these findings. In most qualitative analysis, the interpretation and discussion of the data is an integral part of the analysis. To separate these for the purposes of conforming to a report style more suited to quantitative analysis is pointless and could result in some loss of the richness of the information provided. In qualitative papers, interpretation of the findings is usually supported by direct quotes from participants. Participants are normally given pseudonyms to protect their anonymity but to allow quotes from the same individual to be identified.

Where a separate Discussion section is presented (as will be the case in reports with analysis of quantitative data), the Discussion section should highlight the main findings from the study and discuss how these fit with previous research. That is, there should be a discussion of how the findings of the study correspond with what we would expect, on the basis of existing information, or how the findings contradict existing information. Where contradictions with previous research are apparent, some attempt should be made to explain these. In any case, the Discussion section should address how the study findings advance our knowledge in the area and what the implications of these findings are for future research and/or practice in the area. This discussion can and should take place regardless of whether your findings emerged as you expected. Sometimes trainees appear a little distressed about writing a Discussion section, after conducting quantitative analysis, when they have no statistically significant results to report. If your design and methods are appropriate, then the lack of significant results, when you would not have expected this, is an interesting and important finding and needs to be addressed.

No research study is perfect, and during the course of a research project we often learn lessons which will be valuable for other researchers to know about before planning further research in the area. Therefore, a discussion section will usually contain some information about how the research could be improved. This is not a 'get out of jail card' – it is not a facility to excuse poorly planned research. If a problem could have easily been spotted at the planning stage of the research, then steps should have been taken to deal with it then. Including information in the Discussion section about how the research could be improved is meant to advise and assist other researchers; it is not meant to point out the obvious. Often allied with this part of the Discussion section is a discussion of the limitations of the research. This is not a place for you to highlight every shortcoming of your research project but to indicate the characteristics of your research design which limit the generalisability of your findings. In general, it is expected that these limitations were unavoidable but they are important to note, to ensure that your conclusions are interpreted appropriately by the reader. In other words, the limitations are made clear to make it obvious that you are not trying to make conclusions that go beyond the information provided in your data. My pet hate is reading a Discussion section in which a trainee has written that the conclusions are limited by the small sample size and future research should repeat the study using a larger sample size. A statement like this is completely uninformative (and sometimes not accurate). At the very least, some discussion is required on why a small sample size is limiting in the context of the study and how a larger sample size would help to further address the research question. If it is the case that your study simply did not achieve the sample size that you should have obtained, then that cannot be rectified by stating it as a limitation.

A research report submitted as part of training programme requirements will often also include appendices. These appendices are in place to provide assessors with additional information about your research process and help to demonstrate that you are competent in all aspects of the research process. You should check with your training programme about specific requirements for the format and content of appendices to your research report. Common examples of appendices in a report are a copy of letters providing research governance and ethics approval, copies of any questionnaires or interview schedules used in the research, a technical appendix providing additional information about the data analyses, and a reflective appendix which contains your reflections on your experience of the research process.

In addition to this generic guidance, and the requirements of your training programme, it might be useful to consult published guidelines about reporting research using a specific research design. Mostly developed for medical research, there are a range of guidelines which are helpful when considering the content and structure of your research report. Indeed, when using a research design which is covered by these guidelines, many peer-reviewed journals will require you to follow the structure suggested in these guidelines if you wish to submit your research report for publication by that journal. Some of the more commonly used guidelines are:

- Consolidated Standards for Reporting Trials (CONSORT) – guides the reporting of randomised trials (http://www.consort-statement. org/).

- Transparent Reporting of Evaluations with Nonrandomised Designs (TREND) – guides the reporting of non-randomised trials/quasi-experimental studies, with particular reference to behavioural and public health interventions (http://www.cdc.gov/trendstatement/).
- Workgroup for Intervention Development and Evaluation Research (WIDER) – guides the reporting of behaviour change interventions (http://interventiondesign.co.uk/).
- Strengthening the Reporting of Observational Studies in Epidemiology (STROBE) – guides the reporting of cohort studies, case-control studies and cross-sectional studies (http://www.strobe-statement.org/).
- Checklist for Reporting Results of Internet E-Surveys (CHERRIES) – guides the reporting of internet-based surveys (Eysenbach, 2004).
- Consolidated Criteria for Reporting Qualitative Research (COREQ) – guides the reporting of qualitative studies (Tong, Sainsbury & Craig, 2007). However, see Chapter 6.

Finally, you should proof read your research report. I strongly encourage you to set time aside to allow you to do this. The proliferation of spelling, grammar and punctuation errors in a research report can become annoying for an assessor, and it is probably not advisable to irritate your assessor. One thing which will likely irritate assessors is an inappropriate referencing style. Ensure that your reference list and the citations in your text follow a standard referencing style and that it is adhered to consistently throughout the report. You should also ensure that the citations in your text match the reference list exactly. Check with your supervisor to ensure that you are following the referencing system required by your training programme. In the absence of any specific requirements, I suggest that you follow the American Psychological Association's referencing style, as this is the style used by most psychology journals (see Section 9.1.4).

9.1.2 Who should be named as an author on my research when I submit it to a peer-reviewed journal?

When research is being submitted to a journal, it is being submitted for publication in the public domain, and it is important that the report adequately acknowledges the contribution of everyone involved. This acknowledgement might be in the form of authorship on the paper or as a mention in the acknowledgements section of the paper. The question of who should be named as an author can sometimes create tension, especially as authorship on a research paper might contribute to individuals' job appraisals. It is important to realise that people have given their time to contribute to your research project, and it is likely that their managers will want to see some evidence that this time has been spent productively. The most effective way of dealing with this issue is to clarify and seek agreement (at the proposal stage) about the contribution that people involved in the research are expected to make and how they will be acknowledged in the final research report to be submitted to a journal.

When the number of authors is agreed, the order of authors can also be a point of negotiation. In most psychology journals, the order of authors indicates the relative contribution made by each author to the research. Therefore, the author's position on a paper might also be considered by their employer as an indication of whether their time spent on the research project was time spent productively. In most biomedical journals, the position of first author indicates that this person made the largest contribution to the research (as is the case in psychology journals), but the position of last author is reserved for the person considered to be the research team leader (whereas in most psychology journals, the position of last author is given to the person who made the least contribution to the research). Although these issues might seem trivial, being sensitive and responsive to them is an important part of demonstrating your competence in working within a professional team.

In most cases, authorship is quite straightforward and will normally constitute you and your supervisor(s). The order of authorship will depend on the extent of contribution to the conceptualisation of the research project and the involvement in formulation of the final research paper. It is not solely determined by who was the chief data collector. Some guidelines for the consideration of authorship are provided by Game and West (2007), which have been adopted by the BPS. These are similar to the widely adopted guidelines for authorship on research reports submitted to biomedical journals that have been provided by the International Committee of Medical Journal Editors (http://www.icmje.org/ethical_1author.html).

9.1.3 When should I submit my research report for publication in a peer-reviewed journal?

In most cases, the research report that you submit as part of your training course requirement will need to be amended before being submitted to a journal for publication. Often a trainee will begin a new job shortly after completing their training course, and the demands of this new post results in delays of the submission of a research manuscript to a journal. It is important that research is reported in a timely manner, and you have a professional and ethical responsibility to ensure that you make appropriate efforts to disseminate your research findings as quickly as possible. Therefore, you need to set time aside to allow the conversion of your research report into a manuscript suitable for publication in a peer-reviewed journal. If you believe this will not be possible, then you should discuss this with the other members of the research team as soon as this becomes obvious.

9.1.4 How should I structure my research report when I am submitting it to a peer-reviewed journal?

The structure of a research manuscript for submission to a journal is governed by the specific requirements provided by each journal. Therefore, before deciding how to structure your manuscript, you need to choose the journal that you wish to submit to. Your supervisor should be able to provide some guidance about this. When you have chosen a target journal, check the instructions for authors provided by that journal for advice about the style, structure and format of the manuscript. Most journals provide their instructions for authors on the internet.

Many psychology journals use the American Psychological Association (APA) Publication Manual as the basis for their guidelines about the structure and format of manuscripts, so it is worth becoming familiar with this manual. A helpful summary of the manual can be found at: http://owl.english.purdue.edu/owl/resource/560/01/. One of the main differences between your research report and a manuscript submitted to a journal is likely to be the location of any tables and graphs. For most journals, you are required to place all tables and graphs at the end of your manuscript rather than integrating them with the text in the main body of your report.

9.1.5 What happens to my research report when it is submitted to a peer-reviewed journal?

Again, different journals have different procedures for handling manuscripts. In most cases, your manuscript will be submitted online and will then be assessed by an editor to determine whether the topic is suitable for publication in the journal. If it is deemed suitable, the editor will choose at least two reviewers and will ask these people to provide comments on the manuscript and a recommendation. The recommendation will generally fall into one of three categories: reject, send back to the author for revision or accept without revision. Very few articles are accepted without revision. The editor will then provide a final decision, taking into consideration the reviewers' comments. This decision will usually be communicated to you by email.

If you are asked to make revisions to your manuscript, there will be a time limit for this. You should address each of the reviewers' comments in turn, providing an indication of how you have dealt with their comments in your revised manuscript or providing a reason why you have not. It is likely that your revised manuscript will be reviewed again by the same reviewers, and acceptance of the revised version is not guaranteed.

Receiving a decision that your manuscript has been rejected by a journal can be very deflating, and some of the comments made by reviewers can be annoying. At these times, you need to remember that most, if not all, researchers have experienced this. This does not mean that your research is not good and that it will never be published. Sometimes, your paper will be rejected because it does not fit with the aims of the journal; sometimes it will be rejected because of some errors that you can rectify in a future submission; and sometimes it will be rejected because a reviewer did not read it properly! When you receive notification that your manuscript has been rejected by a journal, your initial reaction will often be to reason that the reviewers did not read the manuscript properly. However, after some reflection, you might realise that the reviewers probably did read the manuscript and perhaps your arguments were not expressed clearly – this can be addressed in an improved version of the manuscript. So I caution against making any decisions immediately after receiving a decision on your manuscript from a journal. I suggest leaving the reviews for a few days and then re-reading them with a different perspective. Whatever the case, do not be disheartened. Journals receive many more manuscripts than they can publish, and rejection of some is inevitable. However, if your research is good quality, then it will be published – it's just a matter of finding the right journal. So if your manuscript is rejected by a journal, consider the reviewers' comments carefully, improve the manuscript accordingly and submit it to another journal.

9.2 Presenting statistical findings

One of the main difficulties that trainees encounter when writing a research report is how to construct the results section of the report. Although the outline structure of a results section has been included in Section 9.1.1, presenting statistical findings throws up some specific dilemmas for the trainee psychologist which require more detailed discussion. Therefore, I have decided to return to a discussion of the results section, to consider specific, recurring queries related to the analysis of quantitative data.

9.2.1 How should I structure a results section?

The obvious thing to include in a Results section of a research report involving quantitative data analysis is the results of the analysis that answers the research questions. This is an essential part of the results section and will be dealt with in more detail in Section 9.2.2. However, in their haste to include this information, trainees sometimes forget that a good Results section usually begins with a description of the sample.

The descriptive statistics will help the reader to form a picture of the sample (in terms of demographic characteristics and the key variables in the study). This will be useful in determining whether the research findings are likely to be applicable to the reader's own situation (for example, whether the participants in the research are similar to clients in the reader's clinical practice). Descriptive statistics are also useful in making sense of further analyses. For example, it might be the case that you find a small correlation between two variables in your study that you would expect to be correlated more strongly. Such a discrepancy might be explained by an examination of the descriptive statistics – if these variables have very low estimates of variance (for example, very low standard deviation values), then this lack of variation could be the reason for the lower-than-expected correlation coefficient.

Before proceeding to the main analysis of your results section, you should include statistical analysis to demonstrate, where possible, how your sample meets some of the study validity criteria. One threat to internal validity that we discussed in Chapter 4 is selection bias, where the control group and intervention group in a study differ at the baseline stage. To demonstrate that selection bias is not likely to be present in your study, you can compare the two groups on their baseline characteristics, using an independent t-test, Mann-Whitney U test or chi-square test, as appropriate.

A threat to external validity discussed in Chapter 4 is the lack of representativeness of your sample. Primarily, this is addressed by the choice of an appropriate sampling technique but statistical analysis demonstrating that the data provided by your sample is similar to previously published good quality data from other samples might provide some reassurance. It is unlikely that you will be able to obtain the raw data in published literature, and, therefore, this analysis will consist of comparing your raw data with summary scores (such as mean values) reported by other researchers. In this situation, the one sample t-test or the one sample chi-square test will be useful.

Even when you have gone to the trouble of undertaking a rigorous sampling procedure, it is possible and likely that some of the people approached to participate in your study will either refuse to participate or will drop out of the study at some point and not provide a full set of data. This latter situation arises more commonly in longitudinal research but can also happen in cross-sectional research when, for example, a research participant does not complete all the scales on a questionnaire. To aid consideration about whether this attrition has biased the sample, you could include analysis that compared those who agreed to participate with those who refused and you could compare those who completed the study with those who did not. Comparing those who agree to participate with those who refuse can be difficult as it might be impossible to obtain any data on the people who refused to participate in the study, but any data you can obtain (in an ethical manner, of course) might be useful.

Overall, your results section should be structured in a clear and coherent manner. It is mostly the presentation of technical information and, therefore, can be repetitive. This is acceptable but there should be a narrative thread running through the results. That is, the reader should be able to follow the logical sequence of the analyses, and you might need to provide some narrative to help them steer a course.

At this point you might be thinking 'why not provide me with an example of a completed results section'. Primarily, I have not provided an example results section because I believe that the pros of doing so are outweighed by the cons. A results section can take many forms and by providing an exemplar, there is a danger of suggesting that there is a single correct format for the presentation of a results section. Your results section will differ depending on what type of analyses you have conducted and the nature of your research questions (which will of course steer the choice of analyses). Alternatively, I have attempted to provide some guidelines to constructing your results section, which aim to be sufficiently generic to allow them to be applied to any form of quantitative analysis.

9.2.2 What analyses should I include?

In addition to the analyses discussed in the previous section, you also need to consider the content of the major analyses in your results section, that is, the analyses that meets the aims of the study.

In my experience, the problem with this part of the results section is that trainees try to include too much information. Faced with a large data set, it is tempting to think of interesting analyses that could be done with the data and before too long you are faced with a mountain of analyses and a lot of confusing information. The way to avoid this is to develop a plan for your analysis. This plan should aim to directly answer your research questions and nothing else. In manuscripts submitted to journals and, possibly, in the research report submitted to your training programme, the amount of space you can devote to the analyses will be limited. Therefore, you must prioritise the analysis that addresses the research questions, as it is unacceptable to omit this analysis.

Of course, it is possible that through the examination of your data, you become aware of other analyses that you believe would be inform-ative and that you want to disseminate to others, but which does not address your original research questions. You should not ignore this information – some of our greatest discoveries have occurred by accident! However, you need to consider whether it is possible to integrate this information into your existing report, while not contravening the space limitations or adversely affecting the coherence of the report, or whether it needs to be addressed in a separate research paper, perhaps even a short report written for a journal.

Overall, the analyses that you include should be meaningful. You should avoid the 'all possible analyses' approach, where statistical tests are generated because they can be. I think sometimes this occurs because trainees are worried that they might overlook some important analysis and therefore include everything. This usually culminates in a confusing set of results where any important findings are buried and often involves the inclusion of findings which are tautologous but which are highlighted because they are statistically significant, even though that is not inter-esting or informative. This is the danger of focusing on the results of the statistical analyses and losing sight of their meaning.

9.2.4 *How do I report the results of statistical tests?*

When reporting the results of a statistical test you need to provide the test value, the p value (or significance level), the degrees of freedom (where appropriate) and a measure of effect size.

Degrees of freedom (df) is basically a way of saying how many scores were involved in calculating your statistic. This is necessary to calibrate the p (or significance) value of your statistic. Some journals will specify how df values should be reported. Therefore, when submitting a research report for publication it is important that you check the manuscript submission guidelines provided by the publisher. Common methods of reporting the test value, df, p value and effect size are to separate the information by commas (for example, $t = 1.622$, $df = 434$, $p = 0.105$, $d = 0.11$) or to include the df in parentheses (for example, $t(434) = 1.622$,

$p = 0.105$, $d = 0.11$). For analyses of variance (ANOVAs), you will need to report two degrees of freedom – one for the 'treatment effect' and one for the error. For example, $F(2, 432) = 4.641$, $p = 0.010$ is the usual method of reporting results from the following ANOVA table:

Table 9.1 An example of an ANOVA table

	Sum of squares	df	Mean square	F	Sig.
Between groups	179.069	2	89.535	4.641	0.010
Within groups	8333.951	432	19.292		
Total	8513.021	434			

Most journals will also specify how p values should be reported, for example the number of decimal places to be reported. It is common for p values to be reported to three decimal places, for example, $p = .003$, $p = .052$, $p = .231$, $p = .092$. Most statistical software packages will provide at least this level of accuracy, however in some cases statistical packages will report a p value as 0.000, and it would be incorrect to state this value in a research report. As it stands $p = .000$ is the same as reporting $p = 0$. Of course, a probability value of zero indicates that there is absolutely no chance of an event occurring, and we can never be that confident about our results. When a computer reports a p value of 0.000 it actually means that the p value is something less than 0.0005 and it becomes 0.000 when it is rounded off to 3 decimal places. In this situation, it makes more sense to report $p < .001$. Yet, reporting $p < .05$ when the p value is anything less than 0.05 and $p > .05$ when the p value is anything greater than 0.05 is not helpful. For example, $p > .05$ is true when $p = .055$ and when $p = .999$. Clearly, there is a large difference between these results, which may well affect your interpretation. Furthermore, providing exact p values in research reports can assist in the conduct of meta-analysis (see Chapter 2).

The results of statistical analyses should be presented in a consistent manner. For example, report results to the same number of decimal places throughout the report, use effect sizes for all analyses (or ensure that information is presented to allow an effect size to be calculated easily), and do not change your treatment of variables between analyses. By this latter point I mean, for example, that if you decide that a variable does not meet the assumptions for using a parametric test in one analysis, then it will seem odd that the same variable is included in a parametric analysis in another instance. At least, this inconsistency will require an explanation.

When reporting the results of a statistical test, you should also add some interpretation. Although this is largely left for the discussion section of a report, some brief interpretation will be helpful in the results section. That is, I think it is useful to indicate the direction of the results presented. For example, informing the reader that there was a large and statistically significant difference found between two groups is only part of the information. It is also necessary to know the direction of this difference, that is, which group scored highest.

9.3 The viva experience

For some readers of this book (most likely many of those enrolled on a MSc in Health Psychology), there will be no viva exam at the end of this period of your training. However, for most trainees undertaking a university-based doctoral level qualification in clinical psychology or health psychology, or the British Psychological Society Qualification in Health Psychology, the viva exam marks the beginning of the end of the research process on a formal training programme. Depending on your training programme, the viva exam might include a discussion/assessment of other competences in addition to research, but at least part of the purpose (if not the sole purpose) of the viva is to provide an opportunity for your assessors to make a final assessment about your competency in research. Although the focus of this book is on the research competence, you should find out what other competences might be assessed during your viva. Understandably, the viva is an anxiety-provoking situation for any trainee, so the aim of this section is to provide some information about the nature of the viva process in order to minimise any anxiety that you experience, to enable you to give your best performance in the viva. It is important to preface the remainder of this section by stating that the viva process will differ based on the regulations of your training programme, the style of your assessor and the approach that you adopt. Consequently, no viva experience is the same as any other. In a way, that is what makes them special. The viva experience is something that you will remember for some time; it is something that is personal to you; and for most of us, it is an important life event, representing the culmination of years of hard work. It represents a very personal rite of passage that I believe has an important role in postgraduate training. Given the status of this event, experiencing some anxiety about it is appropriate. The important thing is to ensure that this anxiety does not prevent you from demonstrating to your assessors that you are a competent, independent researcher.

9.3.1 What happens during a viva?

As I mentioned above, every viva is different, but there are some general procedures that are common to most vivas. In most cases, you will have two assessors. The viva should take the form of a discussion about your research (and any other issues that are covered by vivas within your training programme), with the assessors facilitating this discussion by asking questions and probing for further information. Some assessors will prefer to work through your research report in the order that you have presented the information and some will prefer to deal with issues as they arise during the course of the conversation. Do not be surprised if your assessors provide no indication about their thoughts about your work at the beginning of the viva, as the regulations of some institutions do not allow this.

With regard to the research competence assessed during the viva, you will often be asked to summarise your research (the aims, methods, main findings and conclusions) at the beginning of the viva. Assessors will use this technique to clarify your perception of the research and to give you a chance to speak about something that should come easily to you. In other words, it gives you a chance to become accustomed to the setting of the viva and to become more relaxed.

The time spent during the discussion that forms the viva process is not an indicator of how your assessors view your work. Sometimes assessors will spend a short time with a trainee because their written work is very clear and thorough and there is little left to discuss; sometimes assessors will spend a long time with a trainee because the conversation about the research is engaging and enthuses all parties to participate at length. The outcome for both trainees might be the same. In general, a viva exam will last somewhere between 30 minutes and two hours, partly depending on the volume of work being assessed.

In some situations, the viva will end, and you will be told when to expect a formal decision on the outcome. In these cases, it can be awkward for an assessor to provide you with an indication of the likely outcome, as a discussion needs to take place between the assessors to consider the evidence and make a recommendation to the Board of Examiners (or equivalent). Therefore, the assessors will not want to provide you with an indication of the outcome that later turns out to be different. In other situations, your assessors will ask you to leave the room to allow them to have a discussion and decide on their recommendation to the Board of Examiners. You will then be asked to return to the room, and you will be provided with the provisional outcome and with a brief indication of the reasons for the outcome. This will be followed at a later time by a formal, written decision.

9.3.2 How will my research competence be assessed during the viva?

An alternative to this question is 'How should I prepare for the viva?'

Part of the anxiety associated with the viva stems from the apparent mystery surrounding the assessment criteria and what you need to know before going into the room with your assessors. To some extent, not knowing exactly what you will be asked in a viva is part of the reason for having a viva. The viva is one way of assessing your research competence. If you are competent, then you will be able to provide an adequate answer to most questions asked, without pre-empting them. Therefore, your preparation for the viva has already taken place. By engaging fully in all stages of the research process, by experiencing the highs and lows of this process first hand, and by solving the inevitable problems that every applied researcher faces, you have prepared for the viva. If you have not engaged in the process and learned from the experience, then you have not prepared for the viva, and it is likely you will not be deemed competent in research. Of course, even if you have fully engaged in the research process, it will be beneficial to re-read your research report shortly before your viva, just to remind yourself about the detail of your study.

Basically, your assessors want to know whether you have reached a level of research competence appropriate for the qualification for which you have enrolled. They will be able to make a partial judgement about this on the basis of your written report, which they will read before the viva. However, your assessors will be aware that sometimes the quality of your research is diminished in the written presentation and will know that sometimes things happen that are outside your control and that prevent you from demonstrating your competence fully in a written report. Therefore, the viva is partly about providing you with an opportunity to indicate to your assessors that you can critically evaluate your work and you can indicate alternative courses of action that might have improved the quality of your research.

This critical appraisal must be balanced with an ability to justify why you made the decisions that led to the research product. Assessors will want to know that you can robustly defend your decisions, and therefore you should expect assessors to ask challenging questions in a viva and, perhaps, to take a 'devil's advocate' approach. Remember that your assessors probably enjoy engaging in academic debates about research and do not intend their criticisms to be a personal attack on you or an attempt to discredit your research. They will probably be surprised if you react in a way that indicates that this is your perception. You need to be able to provide a sound rationale to defend your research against these challenges while at the same time acknowledging when things could have been done better. This should happen in a professional, courteous and mutually respectful atmosphere.

9.3.3 What do I do after the viva?

If you are not given a provisional decision about the outcome after your viva, then it can seem like an anti-climax and you will probably be unsure about what to feel. This is an unpleasant situation for assessors and for trainees. Unfortunately, there is nothing you can do except to wait. No matter how many people you tell about the questions you were asked and the answers you gave, the outcome will not be known until the final decision is communicated to you.

When you do find out your viva result, hopefully it will be good news, and you will be able to celebrate a well-earned achievement. The very small drawback is that sometimes you will need to make revisions to your portfolio before it can be finally passed. This is normal and the revisions should not take too long and therefore should not dampen your celebrations. However, remember that there will be a time limit on completing the revisions, so the sooner they are completed, the better. Also remember that this will probably be the time that you need to think about submitting your research to a journal for publication.

Apart from the important task of ensuring that your research makes a contribution to psychological knowledge by seeking publication in a peer-reviewed journal, this is also a good time to make sure that your research is disseminated to other appropriate people, if you have not already done so. Perhaps you promised participants a summary report of your research – if so you should ensure this happens. It is also important to disseminate your findings (in an accessible form) among policy makers, NHS managers, collaborators on the research project and other colleagues as appropriate. In this way, psychological research can inform decisions, policies and practice within health care, and you will be performing a useful service of promoting the role of psychology in the applied health setting. Apart from making a valuable contribution to the profession, you might just create some employment for yourself!

In a way, this is the end of the research process; but it really should be the beginning of your ongoing contribution to psychological knowledge in your chosen field.

References

Ajzen, I. (1985). From intentions to actions: a theory of planned behavior. In J. Kuhl & J. Beckman (eds), *Action-control: From Cognition to Behavior* (pp. 11–39). Heidelberg: Springer.

Altman, D. G. & Bland, J. M. (2005). Treatment allocation by minimisation. *British Medical Journal*, 330, 843.

Atkins, S., Lewin, S., Smith, H., Engel, M., Fretheim, A. & Volmink, J. (2008). Conducting a meta-ethnography of qualitative literature: lessons learnt. *BMC Medical Research Methodology*, 8, 21. http://www.biomedcentral.com/1471-2288/8/21

Barbour, R. S. (2001). Checklists for improving rigour in qualitative research: a case of the tail wagging the dog? *British Medical Journal*, 322, 1115–1117.

Baron, R. M., & Kenny, D. A. (1986). The moderator-mediator variable distinction in social psychological research: Conceptual, strategic and statistical considerations. *Journal of Personality and Social Psychology*, 51, 1173–1182.

Brace, N., Kemp, R. & Snelgar, R. (2009). *SPSS For Psychologists*, 4th edn. London: Palgrave Macmillan.

Braun, V. & Clarke, V. (2006). Using thematic analysis in psychology. *Qualitative Research in Psychology*, 3, 77–101.

Britten, N., Campbell, R., Pope, C., Donovan, J., Morgan, M. & Pill, R. (2002). Using meta ethnography to synthesise qualitative research: a worked example. *Journal of Health Services Research and Policy*, 7, 209–215.

Bulté, I. & Onghena, P. (2009). Randomization tests for multiple baseline designs: An extension of the SCRT-R package. *Behavior Research Methods*, 41, 477–485.

Burns, N. (1989). Standards for qualitative research. *Nursing Science Quarterly*, 2, 45–52.

Carr-Hill, R. A. (1992). The measurement of patient satisfaction. *Journal of Public Health Medicine*, 14, 236–249.

Chamberlain, K. (1999). Using grounded theory in health psychology. In Murray, M. & Chamberlain, K. (eds) *Qualitative Health Psychology Theories and Methods*. London: Sage, pp. 183–201.

Cohen J. (1960). A coefficient of agreement for nominal scales. *Educational and Psychological Measurement*, 20, 37–46.

Cook, T. D. & Campbell, D. T. (1979). *Quasi-experimentation: Design and Analysis Issues for Field Settings*. Chicago: Rand McNally.

Dempster, M., Carney, R. & McClements, R. (2010). Response shift in the assessment of quality of life among people attending cardiac rehabilitation. *British Journal of Health Psychology*, 15, 307–320.

Dixon-Woods, M. & Fitzpatrick, R. (2001). Qualitative research in systematic reviews. *British Medical Journal*, 323, 765–766.

Duval, S. & Tweedie, R. (2000). Trim and fill: A simple funnel-plot-based method of testing and adjusting for publication bias in meta-analysis. *Biometrics*, 56, 455–463.

Eatough, V. & Smith, J.A. (2006). I feel like scrambled egg in my head: an idiographic case study of meaning making and anger using interpretative phenomenological analysis. *Psychology and Psychotherapy: Theory, Research and Practice*, 79, 115–135.

Egger, M., Jüni, P., Bartlett, C., Holenstein, F. & Sterne, J. (2003). How important are comprehensive literature searches and the assessment of trial quality in systematic reviews? *Health Technology Assessment*, 7.

Elliott, R., Fischer, C. T. & Rennie, D. L. (1999). Evolving guidelines for publication of qualitative research studies in psychology and related fields. *British Journal of Clinical Psychology*, 38, 215–229.

Evans, S. (1996). Misleading meta-analysis: Statistician's comment. *British Medical Journal*, 312, 125.

Eysenbach, G. (2004). Improving the quality of web surveys: the checklist for reporting results of internet surveys (CHERRIES). *Journal of Medical Internet Research*, 6, e34.

Field, A. P. (2001). Meta-analysis of correlation coefficients: a monte carlo comparison of fixed- and random-effects methods. *Psychological Methods*, 6, 161–180.

Fleiss, J. L. & Cohen, J. (1973). The equivalence of weighted kappa and the intraclass correlation coefficient as measures of reliability. *Educational and Psychological Measurement*, 33, 613–619.

Form, A. F., Kelly, C. M. & Morgan, A. J. (2007) Participant distress in psychiatric research: a systematic review. *Psychological Medicine*, 37, 917–926.

Gallagher, J. (2008). 'I'm in Limbo'. *Parents' experience of their child's self harm: An interpretive phenomenological analysis*. Thesis submitted as part of the DClinPsych qualification, Queen's University Belfast.

Game, A. & West, M. A. (2007). *Ethical Publishing Principles – A Guideline for Authors*. The British Psychological Society (BPS). Available at: http://www.bpsjournals.co.uk/journals/bjhp/notes-for-contributors.cfm

Glaser, B. G. (1992). *Basics of Grounded Theory Analysis: Emergence Versus Forcing*. Mill Valley, CA: Sociology Press.

Glaser, B. G. & Strauss, A. L. (1967). *The Discovery of Grounded Theory: Strategies for Qualitative Research*. Chicago: Aldine.

Greer, B. & Mulhern, G. (2001). *Making Sense of Data and Statistics in Psychology*. Basingstoke: Palgrave Macmillan.

Griffin, M. G., Resick, P. A., Waldrop, A. E. & Mechanic, M. B. (2003) Participation in trauma research: is there evidence of harm? *Journal of Traumatic Stress*, 16, 221–227.

Harper, D. (in press). Surveying qualitative research teaching on British clinical psychology training programmes 1992–2006: a changing relationship? *Qualitative Research in Psychology*.

Harper, D. & Thompson, A. R. (2011). *Qualitative Research Methods in Mental Health and Psychotherapy: A Guide for Students and Practitioners*. Chichester: Wiley.

Harper, D., O'Connor, J., Self, P. & Stevens, P. (2008). Learning to use discourse analysis on a professional psychology training programme: accounts of supervisees and a supervisor. *Qualitative Research in Psychology*, 5, 192–213.

Heaton, J. (1999). The gaze and visibility of the carer: a Foucauldian analysis of the discourse of informal care. *Sociology of Health & Illness*, 21, 759–777.

Hedges, L. V. & Olkin, I. (1985). *Statistical methods for Meta-Analysis*. Orlando, FL: Academic press.

Hefferon, K., Grealy, M. & Mutrie, N. (2009). Post-traumatic growth and life-threatening physical illness: a systematic review of the qualitative literature. *British Journal of Health Psychology*, 14, 343–378.

Hill, K., Higgins, A., Dempster, M. & McCarthy, A. (2009). Fathers' views and understanding of their roles in families with a child with Acute Lymphoblastic Leukaemia. *Journal of Health Psychology*, 14, 1268–1280.

Horton-Salway, M. (2001). Narrative identities and the management of personal accountability in talk about ME: a discursive psychology approach to illness narrative. *Journal of Health Psychology*, 6, 247–259.

Huck, S. W. (2009). *Statistical Misconceptions*. London: Routledge.

Kraemer, H. C., Kiernan, M., Essex, M. & Kupfer, D. J. (2008). How and why criteria for defining moderators and mediators differ between the Baron & Kenny and MacArthur Approaches. *Health Psychology*, 27, S101–S108.

Lau, J., Ioannidis, J. P. A., Terrin, N., Schmid, C. H. & Olkin, I. (2006). The case of the misleading funnel plot. *British Medical Journal*, 333, 597–600.

López, E. D. S., Eng, E., Randall-David, E. & Robinson, N. (2005). Quality-of-life concerns of African American breast cancer survivors within rural North Carolina: blending the techniques of photovoice and grounded theory. *Qualitative Health Research*, 15, 99–115.

MacKinnon, D. P., Fairchild, A. J. & Fritz, M. S. (2007). Mediation analysis. *Annual Review of Psychology*, 58, 593–614.

McCorry, N. K., Dempster, M., Clarke, C. & Doyle, R. (2009). Adjusting to life after esophagectomy: the experience of survivors and carers. *Qualitative Health Research*, 19, 1485–1494.

McDowell, I. (2006) *Measuring Health: A Guide to Rating Scales and Questionnaires*. 3rd edn. New York: Oxford University Press.

Malone, A., Dempster, M. & Davies, M. (2005). Providing psychological services for people with diabetes. *Practical Diabetes International*, 22, 244–248.

Mertens, D. M. (2010) *Research and Evaluation in Education in Psychology*. London: Sage.

Meyrick, J. (2006). What is good qualitative research? A first step towards a comprehensive approach to judging rigour/quality. *Journal of Health Psychology*, 11, 799–808.

Moher, D., Cook, D. J., Eastwood, S., Olkin, I., Rennie, D. & Stroup, D. F. (1999). Improving the quality of reports of meta-analyses of randomised controlled trials: the QUORUM statement. Quality of reporting of meta-analyses. *Lancet*, 354, 1896–1900.

Moher, D., Liberati, A., Tetzlaff, J., Altman, D. G. & The PRISMA Group. (2009). Preferred Reporting Items for Systematic Reviews and Meta-Analyses: The PRISMA Statement. *British Medical Journal*, 339: b2535.

Mokkink, L. B., Terwee, C. B ., Patrick, D. L., Alonso, J., Stratford, P. W., Knol, D. L., Bouter, L. M. & de Vet, H. C. W. (2010) The COSMIN checklist for assessing the methodological quality of studies on measurement properties of health status measurement instruments: an international Delphi study. *Quality of Life Research*, 19, 539–549.

Morris, S. B. (2008). Estimating effect sizes from pretest-posttest-control group designs. *Organizational Research Methods*, 11, 364–386.

Murray, M. & Chamberlain, K. (eds) (1999). *Qualitative Health Psychology*. London: Sage.

Noblit, G. W. & Hare, R. D. (1988). *Meta-ethnography: Synthesizing Qualitative Studies*. Sage: California.

Noiseux, S. & Ricard, N. (2008). Recovery as perceived by people with schizophrenia, family members and health professionals: a grounded theory. *International Journal of Nursing Studies*, 45, 1148–1162.

NRES (2009). *Defining Research*. Information leaflet from the NHS National Research Ethics Service. http://www.nres.npsa.nhs.uk/applications/apply/is-your-project-research/

O'Sullivan, R. (2003). Focus Groups. In Miller, R. L. & Brewer, J. D. (eds.) *The A-Z of Social Research*. London: Sage, pp. 120–123.

Peel E., Parry O., Douglas M. & Lawton J. (2005). Taking the biscuit? A discursive approach to managing diet in type 2 diabetes. *Journal of Health Psychology*, 10, 779–791.

Perneger, T. V. (1998). What's wrong with Bonferroni adjustments? *British Medical Journal*, 316, 1236–1238.

Peters, J. L., Sutton, A. J., Jones, D. R., Abrams, K. R. & Rushton, L. (2007). Performance of the trim and fill method in the presence of publication bias and between-study heterogeneity. *Statistics in Medicine*, 26, 4544–4562.

Popay, J., Roberts, R., Sowden, A., Petticrew, M., Arai, L., Rodgers, M., Britten, N., Roen, K. & Duffy, S. (2006). *Guidance on the Conduct of Narrative Synthesis in Systematic Reviews*. A Product from the ESRC Methods Programme. Available online at: http://www.lancs.ac.uk/shm/research/nssr/research/dissemination/publications/NS_Synthesis_Guidance_v1.pdf

Potter, J. & Wetherell, M. (1987). *Discourse and Social Psychology: Beyond Attitudes and Behaviour*. London: Sage.

Preacher, K. J., & Hayes, A. F. (2004). SPSS and SAS procedures for estimating indirect effects in simple mediation models. *Behavior Research Methods, Instruments, & Computers*, 36, 717–731.

Preacher, K. J., & Hayes, A. F. (2008). Asymptotic and resampling strategies for assessing and comparing indirect effects in multiple mediator models. *Behavior Research Methods*, 40, 879–891.

Reicher, S. (2000). Against methodolatry: Some comments on Elliott, Fischer and Rennie. *British Journal of Clinical Psychology*, 39, 1–6.

Reid, K., Flowers, P. & Larkin, M. (2005). Exploring lived experience: an introduction to interpretative phenomenological analysis. *The Psychologist*, 18, 20–23.

Rosenthal, R. (1979). The 'File Drawer Problem' and tolerance for null results. *Psychological Bulletin*, 86, 638–641.

Ruzek, J. I. & Zatzick, D. F. (2000). Ethical considerations in research participation among acutely injured trauma survivors: an empirical investigation. *General Hospital Psychiatry*, 22, 27–36.

Smith, J. A. (1996). Beyond the divide between cognition and discourse: using interpretative phenomenological analysis in health psychology. *Psychology & Health*, 11, 261–271.

Smith, J.A. (2004). Reflecting on the development of interpretative phenomenological analysis and its contribution to qualitative research in psychology. *Qualitative Research in Psychology*, 1, 39–54.

Smith J. A. (ed.) (2008). *Qualitative Psychology: A Practical Guide to Research Methods*, 2nd edn. London: Sage.

Smith, J. A., Jarman, M. & Osborn, M. (1999). Doing interpretative phenomenological analysis. In Murray, M. & Chamberlain, K. (eds) *Qualitative Health Psychology Theories and Methods*. London: Sage, pp. 218–240.

Strauss, A. & Corbin, J. (1990). *Basics of Qualitative Research: Grounded Theory Procedures and Techniques*. London: Sage.

Stroup, D. F., Berlin, J. A., Morton, S. C., Olkin, I., Williamson, G. D., Rennie, D., Moher, D., Becker, B. J., Sipe, T. A. & Thacker, S. B. (2000). Meta-analysis of observational studies in epidemiology: a proposal for reporting. Meta-analysis Of Observational Studies in Epidemiology (MOOSE) group. *Journal of the American Medical Association*, 283, 2008–2012.

Tabachnick, B. G. & Fidell, L. S. (2007). *Using Multivariate Statistics*, 5th edn. Boston: Allyn and Bacon.

Taylor, B. J., Dempster, M. & Donnelly, M. (2003). Hidden gems: systematically searching electronic databases for research publications for social work and social care. *British Journal of Social Work*, 33, 423–439.

Taylor, B. J., Dempster, M. & Donnelly, M. (2007). Grading gems: appraising the quality of research for social work and social care. *British Journal of Social Work*, 37, 335–354.

Timlin-Scalera, R. M., Ponterotto, J. G., Blumberg, F. C. & Jackson, M. A. (2003). A grounded theory study of help-seeking behaviours among white male high school students. *Journal of Counseling Psychology*, 50, 339–350.

Todman, J. B. & Dugard, P. (2001). *Single Case and Small n Experimental Designs. A Practical Guide to Randomization Tests*. Mahwah, NJ: Lawrence Erlbaum Associates.

Tong, A., Sainsbury, P. & Craig, J. (2007). Consolidated criteria for reporting qualitative research (COREQ): a 32 item checklist for interviews and focus groups. *International Journal for Quality in Health Care*, 19, 349–357.

Turpin, G., Barley, V., Beail, N., Scaife, J., Slade, P., Smith, J.A. & Walsh, S. (1997). Standards for research projects and theses involving qualitative methods. Suggested guidelines for trainees and courses. *Clinical Psychology Forum*, 108, 3–7.

Wetherell, M. (1998). Positioning and interpretative repertoires: conversation analysis and post-structuralism in dialogue. *Discourse & Society*, 9, 387–412.

Yardley, L. (2000). Dilemmas in qualitative health research. *Psychology & Health*, 15, 215–228.

Yung, Y-F. & Chan, W. (1999). Statistical analyses using bootstrapping: concepts and implementation. In R. H. Hoyle (ed.) *Statistical Strategies For Small Sample Research*. London: Sage, pp. 81–105.

Zaza, S., Wright-De Agüero, L. K., Briss, P. A., Truman, B. I., Hopkins, D. P., Hennessy, M. H., Sosin, D. M., Anderson, L., Carande-Kulis, V. G., Teutsch, S. M. & Pappaioanou, M. (2000). Data collection instrument and procedure for systematic reviews in the Guide to Community Preventive Services. *American Journal of Preventive Medicine*, 18 (Supplement 1), 44–74.

Index